Find Your Happy

Anita Srivastava

Dear Diana,
Wishing you a lifetime of joy,
happiness, love and successes!
Best regards
Anita

Find Your Happy

www.findyourhappybook.com

Publisher
10-10-10 Publishing
Markham, ON, Canada
Printed in the United States of America

ISBN: 978-1542548274

ADVANCE PRAISE for FIND YOUR HAPPY

"I have always believed in empowering individuals whereby we can empower entire communities, societies, nations and the world. There is no better way to do this than encouraging each person to find his/her own path to happiness by breaking down the pattern of negative thoughts and self-sabotaging behaviors. Throughout my years of community building, I have come across several artists and famous personalities. I highly recommend 'Find Your Happy' by Anita Srivastava, as it tells the stories of seemingly ordinary people who have overcome extraordinary obstacles to lead happy, inspiring lives. The book gives you the techniques you can use to overcome obstacles and get your happiness back. They are no less heroes and heroines than famous achievers. It been a pleasure to be acquainted with the talented author, Anita. I hope the message of this book permeates minds and hearts everywhere."

Dr. Romesh Japra, Cardiologist, Founder - Festival of Globe

"To obtain happiness, one must make the right decision and that's a personal choice. Anyone and everyone can be happy, but you must determine what makes you happy, and pursue it vigorously and aggressively. A person must earn the respect of others and obtain knowledge and use of good judgment, and avoid people with a lack for values or judgment in his/her professional and personal life. Each chapter in this book provides solid and proven strategies that will greatly enhance the reader's life. I highly recommend you read it and find your happiness."

Arif Khatib
Founder/President, Multi-Ethnic Sports Hall of Fame,
Moderator: National and International Roundtable
Internet Talk Show

"Find Your Happy" is an engaging collection of stories depicting the triumph of human spirit. How to be more accepting of the life challenges and how to make happiness a habit for life. This book connects us to the life experiences of diverse people and is truly inspirational in helping find strength in distressing times. A happy read towards finding happiness, it provides with the tools and techniques we all can use!
Dr Parveen Kaur, MD

DEDICATION

"Find Your Happy" is lovingly dedicated to my late parents who not only gave me the wings to soar, but also taught me to keep on trying until I succeed.

I would also like to partially dedicate this book to my middle school teacher, Mrs. Samuel, who has been a great inspiration in my life.

FOREWORD

I am impressed with Anita Srivastava's ability to find happiness; no matter what life brings! Whether life gives you lemons or throws you a curve ball, she shows you that there is indeed always a way to *Find Your Happy*. Through this book, Anita shares with you not only how to find joy, but how to maintain it and stay happy!

Find Your Happy is a must read for you. You may be feeling like you are so down that you don't think you can find happiness again, or you may feel that you need a certain *something* or *someone* in order to be happy. Anita shares with you the stories of different people going through life challenges and using their examples, she will teach you how to find happiness despite the struggles *you* may be facing. Through the stories of bullying, incarceration, dealing with breast cancer, and other life changing events, Anita will show you how to find joy even in the darkest situations. She shows you that *what you think* is more important than any diagnosis, more important than the norm. Anita reveals how the right attitude can help you find happiness in any situation. She shares with you that even when others say that there is no hope, your faith, determination and positive life changes will help you find your happiness. This book will change how you think about life, what you think about happiness, and it will provide you with the tools and strategies to find joy. The key learning from each story equips you with techniques to find your mojo and to *Find Your Happy.* It shows you the ways to become happy in life that nothing or no one can take away from you. So, go ahead, learn from Anita and *Find Your Happy*!

Raymond Aaron

New York Times Bestselling Author

CONTENTS

ACKNOWLEDGMENTS

I have been blessed with many amazing people in my life who have motivated, inspired and supported me. I am very grateful to my family, my friends and the ones who trusted me enough to share their life stories for this book. I am especially thankful to my siblings Amrend, Ashish, Anu and Venu for their encouragement and support.

I am very grateful to Lakshmi and Linda for editing my book and providing valuable suggestions.

I would also like to acknowledge Seline, Sheila, Arina, Inna, Maria, Lei, Jaspal, Audrey, Karla, Ryan, Brian, Michael, Kimberly, Steve, Rocky, Dada, KC, Vinnie, Elizabeth, Sudhir, Arif, Dr Japra, Parveen, Brett, Elizabeth, Cara, Dennis, Gowsalya and Aprilani. A big thank you to Allison, Bob, Tony, Cloe, Ken and Alyssia for the inspiration.

I am also grateful to the teachings of Martin Luther King Jr., Rumi, to my Tony Robbins family, and everyone else who supported and inspired me throughout the writing.

.

Anita Srivastava

A Quick Note from the Author

While working in the high tech industry for over a decade, I realized that even though most of my colleagues had the material things such as homes, cars, significant others, kids, fat bank accounts and so on, most of them were stressed out and frustrated. They were yet to find their happy, they were yet to find lasting happiness. They were running from one appointment to another, trying to meet deadlines and barely having time to rest and relax. This led to frustration and stress in some while a few got depressed and thought about taking their own lives.

Seeing so many people needing to 'Find their happy' inspired me to write this book and open my company, Happiness Factor. The organization provides coaching, training and inspiration to empower both individuals & organizations to happiness, motivation, presence and engagement.

The stories in this book are the stories of real people who have gone through tremendous life challenges and had to find happiness again through strength, grit and determination.

Some of the names have been changed to protect the identities of the people. Some of them have asked me to use their real names as they love to share how far they have come in their life; how long their journey has been.

I have shared a couple of my poems in the end. One on gratitude, one on joy. I have also shared pictures from a couple of my stories.

I am looking forward to hearing from the readers of *Find Your Happy*.

To contact the author via email:

findhappy14U@gmail.com

1.
WHAT IS HAPPINESS?

Happiness: What is it? How do we find it? Is it possible to sustain it? What comes to your mind when you think about happiness?

Different people define happiness differently. For a mother, seeing her child smile is happiness, whereas for a child, being praised by the parents is happiness. For an achiever, achieving a goal is happiness, for a lover, being in the arms of his/her beloved, is happiness. For a student, acing the class is happiness, for a player, winning the game is happiness. For an empath, helping others is happiness, for the sick, getting well is happiness. For the patriots, saving the country is happiness, for the kindhearted, an act of kindness is happiness. For a hermit, finding the divine is happiness, for the wronged, getting justice is happiness. For the hungry, having a meal is happiness, for the destitute, getting money is happiness. For the lonely, being with someone is happiness, for the hurting, getting healed is happiness. Being happy is usually synonymous with feeling joyous. Some people associate fulfillment with happiness. In general, everyone agrees that happiness is a positive feeling, which makes people feel good about themselves and their surroundings.

According to Psychology Today, happiness is "More than simply positive mood, happiness is a state of well-being that encompasses living a good life— that is, with a sense of meaning and deep satisfaction." Wikipedia defines happiness as "a mental or emotional state of well-being defined by positive or pleasant emotions ranging from contentment to intense joy. Happy mental states may also reflect judgements by a person about their overall well-being." Sara Algoe and Jonathan Haidt say that "happiness" may be the label for a family of related emotional states, such as joy, amusement, satisfaction, gratification, euphoria, and triumph.

Why do we need to find happiness?

Happiness is the key to our well-being. It not only promotes a sense of well-being, health and healthy habits, it also boosts our immune system, gives us a positive outlook towards life and is integral to being kind, compassionate, loving, affectionate and caring human beings. Many of the world's problems will go away if people found happiness. A happy person does not hurt another human. A happy person will seldom cause harm. The problems of terrorism, depression, wars, killings, espionage, etc. can be avoided if people were happy. A happy person will try to help rather than harm or kill.

Being happy does not mean that you have no issues, no problems in life. Being happy means that you are better equipped to deal with the issues and problems in life. Being happy makes you better equipped to face challenges and make good decisions. Many people think that having money brings happiness or being wealthy brings happiness. If that were true, all billionaires would be the happiest people on earth. Though a certain amount of money is necessary to take care of the basic needs, the more you have, the more you want. There is no limit. Chasing money is an antidote to happiness because of that reason. I have a friend who is in the 6th decade of his life, has never been married, has no kids and has millions. He was from a poor family and was so busy chasing money that he never made time for a relationship. Fast forward to now, he is regretting losing out on love and family in his thirties and his money can't buy him the lost years. He has a ton of money and no loved one to share with. Another scenario is, having money, fame and success, but no fulfillment. That scenario might make someone very unhappy as all the money in the world cannot replace fulfillment. Who hasn't heard of Robin Williams' death? He had the money, fame, success but no happiness. Even though some people think that being famous brings happiness, that's far from the truth. Money, fame or success can bring happiness when accompanied by fulfillment. On their own, they might become meaningless and thus not make any difference to the level of happiness.

Other aspects that affect happiness include the environment, spirituality, lifestyle, family dynamics, contentment and emotional development. Sometimes, people in developing countries might be happier than some living in developed countries, especially in the countries with a team oriented culture.

According to Shareable, the common factors

among the top 10 happiest countries in the world are: subjective wellbeing, jobs and earnings, income and wealth, health status, social connections, environmental quality, education and skills, and personal security. Strong sense of community, civic engagement and satisfaction with life were other key factors to happiness.

Happiness is a state where the positive dominates so much so that it positively affects the life of an individual making him/her more cheerful, optimistic, hopeful, kinder more generous, compassionate, loving. Basically, it impacts the other emotions profoundly. So much so, that we all strive to be happy, we all want happiness as a key ingredient in our lives.

Sometimes, life brings challenges and throws us out of balance. In the stress of dealing with the challenges, it gets difficult to envision being happy. Sometimes, it looks hopeless, sometimes we are ready to give up, sometimes, we are so stuck in the rut that we are not able to see the light at the end of the tunnel. That's when we need to find our happiness that is when we need ways to find our happy.

The stories that follow will give you the various challenges people have gone through in their lives and what we can learn from their stories to find happiness, find our happy.

2.

BARRIERS TO LOVE

Rene was out on a date and the guy, Miles seemed super nice. He was waiting for her outside the restaurant when she arrived a few minutes late because of the traffic. She always tried to be on time, as time is the most precious element that once gone, is gone forever. However, running from one meeting to another, she barely had time to get ready. She wanted to look good, as she had heard so much about Miles. People seemed to like him.

Even though he had initially approached her via a dating site, they seemed to have a few friends in common and all of them had good things to say about him. Not only was he smart, confident and successful, he was also very handsome and caring, the rare combination of looks and maturity! She wanted to look pretty and cute and make a good impression on him. They had been talking over the phone since the past week but this was the first time their schedules matched and made it possible for them to meet.

Miles was waiting patiently for her outside the restaurant when she arrived. He escorted her inside with flair. On their table was the most beautiful bouquet of roses she had seen. He handed them to her and pulled out a chair for her to sit. He had picked a red wine she loved and as they sipped it, the conversation seemed to flow smoothly. He handed her the menu, asking her to select the dishes, saying he would like to share whatever she was having.

When the food arrived, he served her first. She was touched with his manners. How many guys in this day and age know how to treat a woman!

She was enjoying his company and having a good time. Yet, at the back of her mind, she was thinking about Bruce, the guy she felt such a strong connection with, the guy she would do anything for. She had worked with Bruce in the past and didn't realize when she fell for him. They had not dated and she didn't know how he felt. At work, they had had a formal working relationship and that was it. Whenever she saw him sad or stressed out, she felt like comforting him, giving him a hug, wiping the frown from his forehead. She of course made sure no one knew about it, not even him and barely talked to him.

Her getting quiet in his presence was so obvious that he tried to not make too much contact with her. He didn't even know that she loved him. He thought that he might have rubbed her off in a wrong way, for her to not talk to him. So, he gave her space. Anyway, that was way back in the past. Here, she was now moving forward in life and Miles seemed to make the mark. He was funny, witty and kind and seemed totally into her. What more could she want? Yet, he wasn't Bruce. So, on and off during the conversation, she started thinking about Bruce, and had to force herself to get back into the conversation.

Miles seemed to not mind, even though he must have noticed. He was too polite to point it out. He was happily talking and making her smile and she really liked his sense of humor. There was live music, and they danced a little. She didn't seem to mind his arms around her. He walked her to her car and said that he would call her soon.

He texted her immediately saying what a great time he had with her and how much he was looking forward to seeing her again. She was happy with his attention. She also thanked him. Her best friend called her while she was driving back, to ask how the date went. Rene told her how chivalrous, funny and nice

Miles had been. She had had a good time, but she said that she was thinking about Bruce. Sini was her best friend since undergrad and knew her well. She also knew that there was no future with Bruce as he had a serious girlfriend and she was pregnant. She told Rene to forget about him and focus on Miles. It's not every day that you meet a guy who has everything - looks, success, money and chivalry. She asked Rene to give Miles a serious chance.

Sini had seen Rene heartbroken when she had found out about the pregnancy. She had seen her lose interest in everything and everyone. She wanted her to be happy. Rene was a beautiful, successful woman with a kind heart. She deserved a good man, someone who would love her back, who would treat her as a woman of substance should be treated!

So, at her friend's advice, Rene said yes to a second date with Miles. Since she had talked about wanting to ride a hot air balloon, Miles had booked a trip for them. He came to pick her up all dressed up and took her to Sonoma for the balloon ride. She had a lot of fun on the ride and was quite impressed with his charm. He then surprised her with a rooftop five-course dinner at the Castle winery. This guy sure knows how to make a woman feel special, thought Rene. When he kissed her goodnight, she thought about Bruce again and felt the pain in her heart wishing it was him instead of Miles.

When Miles thanked her for another amazing day, she felt bad that even though she was physically there, she was mentally miles away, wondering what Bruce was doing, how he was, whether he was missing her. She told Sini the next day that she wanted to be honest with Miles. She wanted to tell him that she needed to heal, to get her heart back, before she could fall for another guy again, before she could give her heart to someone. Sini advised her to spend some more time with Miles before telling him, hoping that Rene would fall for him.

Rene knew that she needed to take some time off

from dating, to give herself some time to heal. If she was hurting inside, she would bring that pain into the relationship and she didn't want to do that. The way to be happy in a relationship is to be happy inside. Only then will the relationship be happy. When you go into a new relationship while still hurting from the last one, its already doomed.

So, when she met Miles again, she told him what was going on. He was clearly disappointed that she wanted to be friends only for now, but he understood where she was coming from, having been in a similar situation when his wife was killed in a car accident. After a long time, he had met someone whom he thought could make a potential life partner. She was so beautiful, yet was still unspoiled by the world, very honest, pure, an epitome of innocence. Very few women had that nowadays. Most were too much drama, money minded, too shallow, and some were unfaithful. He hoped that she would heal soon, though at the same time he didn't know if he should wait and didn't know how long it would take.

Rene felt relieved after telling him about her pain and also felt a little sad that she wouldn't be seeing him anytime soon. She had enjoyed their time together, had this much fun after a long time.

She went home and cried, cried the whole night asking God why this had to happen to her. Why did she feel so much for Bruce when he didn't even want her? Didn't she deserve to be happy? What had she done wrong? It's not that she consciously fell for Bruce! She realized it only after the fact! She had not asked for that.

Her friends didn't understand this kind of deep love. In their opinion, you only fall in love after you date someone for a while and you know them well. Or with someone who does things for you. Rene had a philosophical bent of mind and she thought that love happens automatically. It's either there or not there. You can't make yourself fall in love! If you try to consciously do it, then it's not love, it convenience. If it's rational, it's not love, it's something else. Her favorite love quote from "Dreams of an insomniac" was, "Unless it's a mad, passionate, crazy kind of love, it's a waste of time. There are too many mediocre things in the world; love should not be one of them."

Dating Miles had made Rene realize that she needed to find ways to make herself heal, to break the connection with Bruce, to shed the barriers she had built against love and allow someone in. She was tired of being alone and was craving to feel loved, to have the companionship, the collaboration of someone close to her heart, someone she could love and who loved her back with all the depth, all the passion, all the romance fairy tales are made of. Maybe someone like Miles, when she was ready.

She hired a coach to help her get emotionally up, started meditation, reading books on Psychology, and started being more aware of why she was feeling the way she was feeling. She made self-development and self-care her top priority. After a few months, she met Kevin with whom she is very much in love with and happily engaged. She is glad that she was able to heal and be happy again.

"Your task is not to seek for love, but merely to seek and find all the barriers within yourself that you have built against it." – Jalaluddin Rumi

Barriers to Love

Key Learnings:

1) Love happens when you are least looking for it.

2) Let yourself heal before starting a new relationship.

3) Deep connections are rare.

4) Sometimes, blessings are disguised to help us grow.

5) Honesty is important.

6) Get into a relationship when you are ready for one.

7) You can have a happy relationship when you are happy inside.

8) True love enters your life once you get rid of the barriers to love.

9) Try to find what patterns are preventing you from getting what you want.

3.

LIVING IN FEAR

Brad did not know what to do. He was so much in love with Julia. For him, it had been love at first sight! Ever since he had set eyes on her a few months ago in a customer service meeting, he could not stop thinking about her. She was so poised, so smart, so beautiful, everything he loved in a woman! She had that rare blend of innocence paired with an I-don't-give-a-damn-what-others-think kind of attitude, yet he could see that she had a kind heart. She went out of her way to help everyone. He tried asking about her life but every time, she would steer the conversation to their client-vendor relationship. It seemed that she wanted to keep it strictly professional.

Also, the timing was off. He had not seen it coming and he wasn't looking for someone. He had recently gotten married to his longtime girlfriend, Bella. He wasn't very sure about getting married to her as they weren't in love but all his friends were having kids and there was pressure on him to start a family as well. Getting married was a natural step towards having kids, he thought, being a responsible man. Since he did not see himself long term with Bella, he had a pre-nup done. They had started trying to get pregnant immediately after getting married. There had been some issues with that and they had decided to go through invitro fertilization (IVF).

He was in a big dilemma. He wanted to leave everything and be with Julia, as nothing would make him happier. Everything was crazy since he had become crazy for her. He was losing interest in everything and obsessing about her. His heart was telling him to risk everything to be with her. But, even though Brad was a highly successful professional, he lived in fear. He was a nice guy but easily manipulated through fear. The sad part was, he wasn't consciously aware of it. His ego would not let him accept that fact.

Even though he wanted her, he was afraid of what people would say. He was too scared to even think about it. He asked his buddy Ken for advice. Ken had been his good friend for a few years and he trusted him. Being aware of how much was at stake, he advised him to not meet Julia and not tell her how he felt. If Brad decided to be with her, he would not only lose his money, but also get estranged from some people he was close to.

Brad trusted Ken and decided to keep his love for Julia a secret within his own heart. Little did he know that this would keep on eating him from inside. He also thought that once he had a baby with Bella, she would not create much fuss about getting divorced. Brad and Bella had gotten married on the premise of having babies. They weren't in love with each other. Brad did not think for a moment that Bella wanted to never let him go as he had been fooled by her fake nice behavior. After all, she had been nice to him! What he didn't realize was that Bella used niceness when necessary, to manipulate people into doing what she wanted them to do. She had average looks and the only way she had kept Brad with her for so long was by pretending to be super nice whenever the situation required. He wasn't very intuitive and never realized the agenda behind the behavior.

Julia, on the other hand, had been with John for a very long time. She had known him since they were teenagers. Over the years, they had become best friends and then lovers. He had started getting a little too possessive about her lately, and she was feeling suffocated. She needed some space but he was not willing to give that to her, afraid that if he did, she might not be with him anymore.

She could not understand why, but she felt a strong attraction towards Brad. She wanted to make him happy; she wanted him close to her. Given the fact that he was a married guy, she decided to hide her feelings and started avoiding him as much as possible so that he would not notice. She was committed to John and Brad was a married guy, trying to have a family. It just wasn't right.

Meanwhile, Brad and Bella had a successful IVF and she got pregnant. It wasn't the most opportune time for him to think about another woman. Also, if he divorced after a few years, the prenup time would be up and he would be able to keep his fortune. Even though he tried to hide it, his feelings for Julia were so strong that he thought about her day and night. He lost interest in everything else and carried on his daily life mechanically. One night, he was dreaming about her, dreaming about making love to her. The dream was so real that he woke up calling out her name.

That was when Bella thought that he was having an affair. He had told her that he was in love with another woman but she was still able to convince him to go through with the IVF. She knew that she would not be able to find another guy like him. She knew how to manipulate him and was aware that he lived in fear. So, she had told him that if he let her have the baby, she would divorce him and he would be free, while making sure that she did not put anything in writing.

When Julia heard about the pregnancy, she was glad that she had kept her distance from him. She did not want to be labeled as a home breaker. If he really loved her, he would have tried to win her over.

They both did not realize how deep their connection was. It was almost as if they were telepathically connected, they could pretty much feel what was happening in each other's lives, even though they were not physically together. Mentally, they weren't even a second away from each other and felt very deeply about one another.

Meanwhile, pressure was mounting on Brad to get more involved with the pregnancy, to help decorate the nursery. Even though he had not discussed with his family, they all could see the change in him. He would get lost in thoughts even in the middle of conversations.

At her end, Julia felt guilty that she was not in love with John anymore and they broke off. She wanted the kind of connection that she had with Brad, with someone who was available. Someone who would treat her the way she deserved to be treated. Someone who would cherish her and love her.

Brad was blessed with a baby girl and he asked Bella to honor her promise and divorce him but she would not hear of it. She and her brother Sam threatened to harass Julia if he met her. Also, they played on his fear that, if he told Julia he loved her, why would she even believe him, when he had just had a daughter with another woman?

Also, the prenup was valid for a couple of years more. So, Brad, on Ken's advice, decided to suck it up and not file for a divorce, even though he and Bella were unofficially separated. He thought that if he was nice enough to Bella, she would feel sorry for him and divorce him. After all, he had kept his part of the promise and gotten her pregnant. She then told him that if he stayed till the first birthday of their daughter, she would then file. Being an honest person himself, he believed her. He had some common friends with Julia and kept track of her, though he did not do the most important thing that would have made all the difference - he never told her that he loved her.

Since Brad wasn't dating anyone, Bella thought that she could get him to be with her again if she could just get him to have sex with her. So, for his birthday, she bought him a vacation package to Oahu. When he was hesitant, she told him that after the vacation, if he still wanted to divorce, she would file for it. He then agreed and they went on vacation. He wasn't attracted to her in spite of the romantic surroundings. His heart was with Julia.

When they came back, he again reminded Bella of her promise. Since this time his parents were also involved, she agreed to file after a few months. Meanwhile, unknown to him, she was undergoing fertility treatment. She made plans to hang out with him and their daughter every time she was ovulating.

Brad was getting more and more despondent that Julia hadn't reached out to him in spite of being single. What he did not realize is that if only he had told her how he felt, she would have left everything to be with him. She was keeping her distance from him.

One of the days he felt so bad that after a day out with the daughter, he agreed to have wine with Bella. They kept on drinking till he was too drunk to really think clearly and ended up having sex with her. He repented it the next day but it was too late. Bella was pregnant a month later. He thought of meeting Julia but then was told that the child had a sixth chromosome and might die during pregnancy or birth. So, he decided to hold off and wait for the dreaded news that would be a blessing in disguise for him, as it would lead to freedom.

When the nine months were up, Bella convinced him to come to the hospital for the birth, saying he should see the baby boy before the baby died. He felt responsible and went to hold the baby and took lots of pictures. After all, babies with the sixth chromosome die before their first birthday. Unknown to him, the baby was normal and Bella knew Brad would leave as soon as he figured it out. She had six months before the baby would start sitting up, before everyone would know the truth.

She could not bear to lose her control over Brad. The only way to keep him was to get him legally bound to her in some way. She pretended she was depressed. Every time he was around, she would just stare at the baby and cry. After a few months, he started believing that she was depressed and that the baby would die sooner than later. Meanwhile, she told him that if he stayed with her till the baby died, she would give him 100% custody of the daughter when they divorced. If he filed for divorce before the baby died, he would lose total custody of their daughter. He thought that he had nothing to lose. He had already waited so many years so another few months wouldn't make that much of a difference. And he would be able to have his daughter with him. So, he signed the papers; signed his life away.

After a few months, he got the shock of his life when the baby started crawling. That's when he realized that he had been played. Even though that made him mad, the fear of losing his daughter kept him from filing for divorce and he continued being controlled by his narcissistic partner.

His male ego combined with the fear of losing the apple of his eye kept him tied to the dead relationship. He started getting sick more often and started drinking more. If he had only been brave enough to get out of his comfort zone, brave enough to face his fears, he would have a totally different life full of love, fulfillment and happiness.

"You gain strength, courage, and confidence by every experience in which you really stop to look fear in the face. You must do the thing which you think you cannot do."

-Eleanor Roosevelt

Living in Fear

Key Learnings:

1) Living in fear is the antidote to happiness.

2) Marriage of convenience is not a happy place to be.

3) Get out of your comfort zone.

4) Learn to differentiate between really nice people and fake nice people.

5) Don't expect different results if you are doing the same thing again and again.

6) Love is the strongest of all emotions.

7) Your decisions decide what kind of life you will have.

8) When nothing seems to work, let go of everything.

9) Be aware of narcissistic behavior and learn to save yourself.

10) Don't trust blindly, seek expert help.

4.

Control and Codependence

Jackie was on the seventh cloud! She had recently started dating Scott and he seemed to be her dream come true! Not only was he suave and charming, he was very courteous and found her to be the most beautiful woman on earth! The previous day when they were out it had started raining. While they were walking back to the car, there was a puddle on the way. He put his jacket on it, so that her shoes didn't get dirty! That had really touched her to the core! No guy had ever done that for her before. Scott seemed to love everything about her. He loved her toned, supple body, her long, wavy hair and big blue eyes, deep like the ocean.

He liked her so much that he wanted to meet her every day. At first she resisted, but since she had so much fun when she was with him, she started wanting to spend as much time with him as she could spare. Soon, they became inseparable. Then, it only made sense that they should move in together, and they did. She barely had time for her friends. Most of her available time was spent with Scott. She used to go on weekly girls' night out regularly before, but the last time she went, Scott missed her so much, he was calling her every fifteen minutes till she returned back and he made her feel guilty for leaving him alone in the house. Her friends commented that he seemed like the jealous type, and when she asked him, he said that it was only because he loved her so much and missed her company. She was reassured after hearing that and felt sorry that she made his sad. After all, he loved her so much! His life revolved around her.

Scott was not a very social person and had very few friends. The ones he was close to were from his engineering school. Larry was the closest one, while Ben and Sven were the other two. They all usually liked to spend the weekend together, and Jackie became a part of their gang soon. Scott didn't really want to hang out with anyone without her, not even his friends. He told everyone how much she meant to him, that he would die without her. He bought her expensive gifts, kissed and hugged her every time they were out. He really liked the public display of affection and making everyone aware that she was his, she belonged to him.

After a few months of living together, Jackie started noticing Scott's moodiness especially after she got promoted and got put on the board of her company. He started blaming her for every little thing, sometimes even in front of his friends. Also, he started putting her down, especially whenever she got more successful or was praised for her work or if some guy complemented her.

On a particular Wednesday, she had a very important meeting with a senior executive. She was so excited that she told Scott about it. On that Wednesday morning, he started getting mad at her without any particular reason. When she tried to talk to him, he started crying, saying that she did not want to be seen with him, that she did not think he was good enough for her.

She had no idea where this came from. She didn't know why he would say that and since they both needed to go to work, so she did not have the time to deal with it then. She was so drained by the time she reached the meeting that she could not really contribute much. Her day was miserable. She was feeling listless.

When she returned home in the evening and wanted to pick up the conversation, he really wasn't in the mood and convinced her to watch a movie with him instead.

On Sunday, she went with Scott to the gym. While he worked out on his own, she had a personal trainer teach her some exercises. Once they were done, they went to the grocery store next door. While they were walking out, suddenly, without warning, Scott got into one of his moods and started shouting at her, while stomping his feet and throwing his phone on the floor. She was astonished and a little embarrassed as people were looking at them. She tried to calm him down and requested him to go home as she picked up the phone. He did not want to drive. She asked him to sit in the passenger seat and started the car.

As she started driving, he started shouting again while threatening to jump out of the car and trying to snatch up the steering wheel. She was afraid they would get into an accident but thankfully, they reached home without any mishap. She was feeling drained and a little upset at his behavior, which she thought was pretty childish. She told him that she would stop talking with him until he apologized for creating the unnecessary scene.

That made him even more moody. He wasn't ready to apologize. He did not think that he had done anything wrong. He took out a pack of cigarettes and started smoking. She decided not to pay attention to that and quietly texted Ben to come over as she did not want Scott to get mad if she called. Ben responded that he was anyway on the way to their house as he had forgotten his iPad at their place.

When Scott smoked a few of the cigarettes and she didn't go to get him as he expected, he came in, caught her by the hand and lay face down on the bed crying that she didn't like him, she didn't love him, that she loved her friends more and so on and so forth. She tried to break free of his grip but he wouldn't let her leave the bed. Meanwhile, Ben was knocking at the door. She wanted to open the door but Scott wasn't willing to let go of her wrist. His grip was so tight that it was hurting her. He started cursing and calling her names, saying that she must have called someone to see him like in that state, that she wanted people to not like him, that she was trying to give him a bad name.

Ben kept on knocking and got a little worried when no one answered after 15 minutes. He decided to enter their home via the backyard garden gate and entered, calling their names. Seeing him there surprised Scott so much that he let go of her hand and she immediately scooted away and opened the door.

Ben started talking to Scott to calm him down. Scott started shouting that Ben was not welcome and should leave immediately. When Ben got up to leave, Jackie pleaded with him to stay, saying she could not handle Scott's moods and needed his help. So, Ben stayed and tried talking with Scott. The more he tried to pacify him, the angrier Scott got and started calling Jackie names and ordered her to get back saying she couldn't escape.

Jackie tried to ignore that by going into the kitchen to get a drink for Ben. When she went to give Ben the drink, Scott got angrier and kicked her. She fell down wincing in pain. Ben was aghast and asked Jackie if he should call 911 but Jackie said no as Scott started crying, saying he did not want to go to jail and that he would never do it again. She let it go as she thought about how much he loved her.

It had happened in the past as well. Whenever Scott's mood got the better of him and he lashed out and hit Jackie, he would start crying and apologizing and that made Jackie feel sorry for him. Instead of getting angry at him for his abusive behavior, she would try to console him so that he would stop crying. She had tried talking about his behavior to one of her friends but he convinced her that these matters should remain amongst the two of them, others should not know about it. He did not want anyone gossiping about them.

Recently, Scott had started buying a lot of meat

cutting knives. That scared Jackie. But then she thought, Scott loves me, he would never hurt me. Recently, he had bought her a shiny new luxury car and a very expensive diamond necklace from Tiffany. Still, she felt uneasy. Uneasy enough to seek out a therapist. She shared the details with the therapist and the therapist said that Scott might be planning to kill her. Also, she said that Scott seemed to have a narcissistic, manipulative, controlling personality and could do anything to keep the control. Jackie could not believe that. This was the guy she loved. He needed her. He couldn't live without her. But she had to agree that recently, his mood swings were getting worse and she did not know what triggered them.

Going through therapy, she also realized that by always trying to fix Scott's behavior, she was codependent on him too. This situation wasn't functional at all. Even though she didn't want to, she needed to find a way out. She needed to find the courage to end the dysfunctional relationship.

Recently, she had transferred her money into the joint account. Scott managed the accounts and the investments.

Even though her heart broke at the very thought of leaving Scott and what would happen to him, she knew that she needed to find an exit strategy. In the past, when she had gotten upset about his abusive behavior and told him that she would leave if he didn't behave well, he had threatened to kill both her and himself and set the house on fire. Even though she knew she needed to leave, she was still very worried about what would happen to him, when she did.

She did not even know how she would manage to live alone. For the past several years, she hadn't really had a life without Scott. They had been doing everything together and since she wasn't allowed to have any friends he didn't know, she barely had anyone she could trust. Sometimes she wondered if dying might be better. But, she was never a coward and with the help of the therapist, was able to muster enough courage to leave and get a restraining order.

Even though she left him, she still felt guilty. She felt guilty that she could not make it work, that she gave up. Maybe he would improve; maybe it was her fault that he abused her. She had all kinds of crazy thoughts.

Meanwhile, since he could not control Jackie anymore, Scott found another woman. He was also able to manipulate Jackie financially and emotionally and she had to find the strength within herself to not just survive but build her life from scratch, putting all the broken pieces together. She was lucky to be able to get out without being too emotionally scarred.

"Since [narcissists] deep down feel themselves to be faultless, it is inevitable that when they are in conflict with the world they will invariably perceive the conflict as the world's fault."

—*M. Scott Peck*

Control **and** Codependence

Key learnings:

1) If someone tries to control everything, it's not love, it's narcissism.

2) Trust is an integral part of love.

3) Abuse is not love.

4) Domestic violence is not your fault.

5) Seek help to get emotionally strong.

6) Codependency is not good for either party.

7) For a healthy relationship, both need to have some interests of their own.

8) Little space in a relationship is healthy.

9) Don't give in to emotional blackmail.

10) Threat is not love.

11) When someone really loves you, they won't hurt you.

12) Emotional blackmail is a tool used by narcissists. Be aware of it.

5.

Duh to Disability

Joey was ecstatic! He had been dreaming about this day for a very long time. He had been saving up, adding every cent he could spare for the last four years. This year, his dream was finally coming true! He was on his way to get his dream ride, his very own Harley Road King. He had thought he would have to wait another few months, based on his savings. But the big bonus came as a pleasant surprise and made it possible now.

He felt so good when he got the keys in his hands! He was on cloud nine, totally in his masculine self and could feel the adrenaline rush as he started driving it home. He was thinking how much fun it would be to ride it on the weekend with his friends.

Joel was Joey's best friend for the longest time even though they had vastly different personalities. While Joey was a clean shaven, white collar, 180 LB professional climbing up the corporate ladder, Joel was a tall, big, heavily tattooed guy with a ponytail whose likes included riding on his Harley, rum and hot women. Both of them had known each other since high school and were very good friends even now. Joey had been inspired to buy his bike because of Joel. Joel loved his bike and took every opportunity to take it for a spin. They had already decided to go riding on the weekend and Joey was excited with the anticipation.

When Saturday came, Joey and Joel, along with a couple of other bikers, decided to go for a joy ride.

They were having a great time as the roads weren't too crowded and the weather was sunny and warm. As there wasn't much traffic to be seen, they decided to race each other around the hills. Suddenly, as they were going around a bend, they saw a big truck coming from the opposite direction at full speed. They signaled each other to go to the side to avoid getting hit. While the other three swerved towards the right side, Joey panicked. Nervousness kicked in while he tried to veer his bike uphill. The bike began to splutter and he went into the wrong gear! He downshifted in panic, released the clutch lever too quickly, resulting in the bike lurching dangerously and falling to the ground, along with him. As his head hit the ground, he had such a searing pain in his body that he almost lost consciousness.

He vaguely heard the helmet hitting the pavement while the screeching sound of the truck tires stopped a few inches away from his neck. He barely heard his friends calling his name while rushing over to his side and thought he was in a dream he would soon wake up from. The sirens of the police, the firetruck and the ambulance seemed to have a hazy, dreamlike quality. He was going in and out of consciousness. The paramedic was slapping his face, trying to keep him awake so as to stop him from going into a coma.

When he woke up days later, he could not move. He was sore all over and his body was covered in bandages. Everything hurt badly. The doctors told him that it was a miracle that he was still alive after such serious injuries from the accident.

With the impact of the accident, he had broken his back, his right arm, punctured both his lungs and one fourth of his head was a big scab.

Seeing the gloomy looks on the faces of his friends and his girlfriend, he thought he was going to die. But in his mind, he was not ready to die yet. He was thinking, "I am only 28 years old; I haven't lived my life yet. I haven't visited the places I want to see, I haven't tasted the different cuisines I want to try, haven't seen how the rest of the world lives, haven't experienced the different cultures. I don't want to die before living fully."

The doctors also found that he had a spinal cord injury. That was perhaps the worst as only the tests would show if he would ever be able to walk again. They poked needles to check his nerves and the results were dreary. The nerves were dead! The diagnosis stated that he would not be able to sit without assistance again and would never be able to walk. They were also afraid that his right arm wouldn't be able to function at all and he would never be able to use it again - the nurse told him about the result of the diagnosis as she pushed his wheel chair.

Even though he was devastated with the diagnosis and the reality check the nurse was giving him, Joey was thinking inside! They don't know me! They don't know my determination! I am honor! I am love! I am loyalty! I am courage! I am unstoppable! He kept on repeating internally to himself while tears

streamed down his face and he was determined!
Determined to prove them wrong! Determined to
heal! Determined that he would not only start sitting
without assistance, he would also start walking, he
would start using his right arm and he would start
living life on his own terms again.

The doctors needed to do a MRI as he was also
diagnosed with brachial plexus injury. Brachial
plexus is a network of nerves formed by the anterior
rami of the lower four cervical nerves and
first thoracic nerve and extends from the spinal cord,
through the cervicoaxillary canal in the neck, over the
first rib, and into the armpit. It
supplies afferent and efferent nerve fibers to the
chest, shoulder, arm and hand.

It took several weeks to get the MRI and other
tests done. By this time, he had started sitting on his
chair to pee in a big jug and the doctors were so
surprised that they could not believe it and called it a
medical miracle, something they had never seen

before. Joey was feeling happy inside, glad that he had started proving them wrong. He was one step closer to living life on his terms. His determination was proving that it was possible for him to get on the path to full recovery, the way he wanted to and do the things healthy people take for granted, such as walking and working out.

When Joey went to the physical therapist for the first time, he told them that he would start walking soon. The physical therapist pitied him while giving him the reality check that "there is optimism and then there is reality." Joey decided to take this with a grain of salt. After all, they did not understand his determination to get well. He was determined to start walking and then go back to working out and build his muscles, no matter what the doctors or the physical therapists said.

His optimistic attitude impressed others and during subsequent visits, the physical therapist mentioned that everyone was talking about him;

about his confidence that he would not only start walking but also start using his arm again, pretty soon.

The doctors had put Joey on heavy nerve medications. Knowing their side effects, Joey decided to quit them cold turkey as soon as he was able to bear the pain and kept his motivation up by watching "Braveheart" every single night. The movie was very symbolic to him as it made him certain that he wouldn't take the bullshit from the doctors about his condition. It also helped him with emotional strength by motivating him to feel that what he was doing was right.

Even though his pain threshold was quite high, he was in a lot of pain. His back hurt so bad that he was ready to pass out. He was living in a recliner, peeing in a jug and eating whatever people brought for him. In spite of these constraints, he did not indulge in pity party. Not once did he feel sorry for himself. His determination to get back to normal, kept him going.

Most of the food people brought for him was unhealthy - mainly burgers, pizza and hotdogs that made his weight shoot up to a whopping 260 LBs, a gain of 80LBs since his accident! He was still confident that once he recovered, he would eat healthy and work out to lose the extra weight and get back in shape.

At times the pain got so bad that he could not even speak; he could only make noises like an animal. Still, his determination to succeed kept him going. He so badly wanted to move forward in life and get well again to live the life he wanted to live, do the things he wanted to do, gain the experiences he wanted to gain, that it kept him going on and focusing on the end goal of healing, rather than the suffering from the pain.

The doctors still thought otherwise. They were still not convinced that he would ever get out of the wheel chair and told him to apply for disability, which he would easily qualify for. But Joey's gut told him not to apply for it. He felt it deep down that he would recover, that he would be his old self again.

It took close to a year, but his grit, determination and the will to succeed kept on propelling him towards recovery. He still gets full of glee when he remembers the shock on his doctor's face when Instead of going in a wheelchair, he walked in for his appointment.

After Joey was able to start using his arms again, he kept his promise to himself to get back to his healthy self. He started working out, eating healthy and even took up a physical job in the oil industry to prove that his limbs were strong again.

He wasn't a quitter and he proved not only to himself and the doctors, but also to everyone around him that how and what you think in your mind is more important in how your life turns around, more that any diagnosis. What you think is what you become! The only limit you have is the limit you put on yourself.

As Henry Ford said, *"Whether you think you can, or you think you can't – you're right "*

Duh to Disability

Key learnings:

1) Always drive safe.

2) Believe your gut, it's your subconscious talking.

3) Unwavering determination and motivation can help you achieve anything.

4) Positive outlook can work miracles.

5) No matter what your current situation, you can always get to a place of strength.

6) When the prognosis looks bleak, find something inspirational to hold onto.

7) Always read the side effects of your medications.

8) Adopt a healthy lifestyle - eat healthy and work out.

9) What you focus on becomes a part of your life.

10) What you think about is what you become.

11) You can get through any accidents and recover if you set your mind to it.

12) When the current situation looks dire, think of the end goal to keep yourself motivated.

.

6.

Entitlement to Maturity

Rally was an only child. She was the apple of the eye for her parents and all her wishes were fulfilled before she asked. Her parents loved her to death and treated her like a princess. She was totally spoilt as a kid and having everything provided for, she grew up with a sense of entitlement. As she grew a little older and sometimes when her parents didn't give her something immediately, she threw tantrums and as they couldn't bear to see her crying, they gave in to her every time. She started using it to her advantage and got conditioned to getting what she wanted this way, if she couldn't get it by asking. She did not get used to getting no for anything she wanted and felt entitled to get whatever she fancied.

When we are young, tantrums are sometimes viewed as cute by the adults around us. It's a good idea to get rid of these tantrums as we grow up and learn the art of being patient and mature enough to accept that sometimes we might not get what we want and that's okay. Sometimes though, we get so conditioned to getting things through tantrums that we keep on throwing them to get what we want, we just learn to be subtler and end up becoming a drama queens, making the life of those who care for us, difficult. That was the case with Rally!

She grew up with a sense of entitlement. After all, she was the best, she was the princess. People should acknowledge that. She failed to learn that each human is special in his/her own way and other people and their needs are equally important as well.

When she moved out of her parents' house in her twenties, she had a very tough time adjusting with other people. She got depressed whenever she could not get what she wanted, whether it was a dress, or a class or a job or a guy. After all, she was the best, her parents always told her that. So, why didn't other people understand how special she was? Why didn't people see her uniqueness? Why didn't they treat her as such?

When she was 23 years old, she saw a black dress in the window of a shop. She really wanted that dress but the designer had made it for a client and told her that it would take him a couple of months to make one for her. She tried convincing him to sell the dress to her, even cried but that didn't help, as he did not have the resources or time to make another one sooner. Though this would not have been a big deal for a mature person, for Rally, it was enough to make her feel as if her world was falling apart that set her on a spiral of depression. This was the tipping point since she had started living on her own and things did not always end up the way she wanted them to. Her doctor prescribed anti-depressants.

After a few months, Rally met Ron and they hit it off immediately. After dating for three years, he popped the question and they got married. They were both young and had a decent life even though they did not have too much wealth. Rally had finished her degree and started working in an ad agency. Ron was finishing his graduate degree. Ron liked to budget but she liked to buy everything that caught her fancy. Whenever Ron talked to her about it, she would say that her parents always bought whatever she wanted. If he loved her, he would do that too. After hearing that, he did not feel like saying anything more. He was getting a bit dissatisfied by her immature behavior though and didn't like the increasing debt on them. Whenever he tried to make her see reason, she wasn't willing to see it and would say things like, she was not born to live like a poor woman. She was meant to be a princess.

One day, he was so fed up with the situation that he suggested separation. Initially, she started thinking: How could Ron be so selfish? Why would he want to leave her? Did he have another woman?

She cried, she begged him to stay, but his mind was made up. She still didn't see that her behavior was driving him away. She put the blame on him.

She was totally devastated. She fell into deep depression. So much that she lost the will to live and started thinking about ways to kill herself. Would it work if she went hiking on a mountain and jumped off the top? Or would it be better to buy rat poison and eat it, or get a gun and shoot herself? Or should cut her hand in the tub and bleed to death?

Luckily, she had an appointment with her shrink and the shrink was able to stop her from committing suicide.

The shock of Ron leaving her and her subsequent

reaction to it and the counseling sessions made Rally gradually realize that sometimes whatever you do, you might not get what you want. It's okay and that's how life is for everyone. That realization totally changed her perspective on life. She started making efforts to help others who were less fortunate. That made her feel so good that she started taking care of herself, working out regularly, taking walks in nature and hanging out with happy people. Changing her habits changed her state so much that within a few months, she was able to wean herself off the antidepressants. She was happier and easier to get along.

Her changed attitude helped her make more friends and also brought Randy into her life who she later realized, was her soulmate. They got married and were blessed with a couple of kids. Rally made sure that her love did not spoil them. She taught them the right values of patience, care, compassion, self-discipline and understanding so that they would have the tools to deal with whatever life brought them when she was not around.

Even though it took her so many years to figure it out, major heartbreak and going to the lowest level in life, once she owned her part in her unhappiness, she was finally at peace. She always had a good heart but her sense of entitlement had covered it with ego and had made her hard to get along with. Now she was happy with her newfound understanding, kindness and thoughtfulness, and her changed attitude made others happy too, including her aging parents.

"Man is not, by nature, deserving of all that he wants. When we think that we are automatically entitled to something, that is when we start walking all over others to get it."

— **Criss Jami**

Entitlement to Maturity

Key learnings:

I. Entitlement needs to be rid of; it's not a good habit.

II. Practice gratitude instead of entitlement.

III. Don't always give in to your kids' tantrums to avoid giving them the wrong conditioning.

IV. Teach good values to your kids to help them once they grow up.

V. Learn to be happy with simple things.

VI. Get rid of drama and expectation.

VII. Don't be too selfish. Think about other people's happiness as well.

VIII. Be thoughtful towards others, try to understand where they are coming from.

IX. Give positive reinforcement instead of negative reinforcement.

X. Give the gift of reading.

XI. Set good examples.

7.

For the Love of my Kids

It was 2012 and Ryan had a good life. He was happy and content with his achievements. He had a good career, nice houses, beautiful wife, luxury sports cars, Harley and a truck. He was leading IT Security for a Fortune 50 employer and traveling around the world. He was also into self-development and had attended trainings and seminars with well-known speakers including Tony Robbins and Brendon Burchard. He was trained in Neuro-Linguistic Programming, too, and was unstoppable. There was nothing he could not achieve. He was flying high and enjoying life! His days began at 5am. He was ready to conquer the world!

He had met this beautiful woman, had a whirlwind romance and the relationship was the one thing he really wanted in life. They were in love, decided to get married and have a family. He was bridging the gaps in his life quickly.

When Ryan and his wife tried to get pregnant, the doctor was not very positive about the outcome as his wife had PCOS (polycystic ovarian syndrome), which was quite painful and she was already 35 years old.

Ryan believed in holistic medicine and knew a well-regarded Chinese traditional medicine practitioner who prescribed medicinal teas to help them. Soon after, she was pregnant. Ryan had a gut feeling that he would have twins even though others thought otherwise. His family had a history of having twins. He has identical twin aunts.

When they went for an ultrasound, there was a little black area in the scan report. When asked, the doctors didn't think it was another baby. As it turned out later, it was the other twin.

It was an incredible miracle for the family when Ryan and his wife were blessed with identical twin boys.

The pregnancy was a very difficult one and his wife had to be rushed to the hospital several times and was put on bed rest. She had to quit her job to carry the pregnancy through and that was not very easy. They tried to make it work as they both wanted kids. That was the time when they made a great couple. She was peaceful; he was energy; she was certainty; he was uncertainty. Everyone around them was happy about the pregnancy.

The babies were born 2 months premature at 7 months old, via a natural birth. He was present for the birth. His wife gave birth while squeezing onto him. Post-delivery, they were in the hospital for two months and she was wheelchair bound for some time.

Florida, where they lived at the time, was not too good when it came to hospital rules for premature birth. The hospital staff did not want to keep the babies with the parents so Ryan had to fight with the hospital a lot, asking them to keep the babies with them. He stayed at the Ronald McDonald House near the hospital.

After a while. he got the children out with them. The mother was confined to a wheelchair for a couple of weeks. He would push the wheelchair to the hospital every day, keeping things together by himself. Her family was not very involved at this time and his mom came to help after his wife gave the okay.

The dynamic changed after the birth of his twin sons. Complications of the pregnancy had his wife leave her job. She was on bed rest and he helped.

They had initially planned to move to Washington for the birth but because of complications and the high risk, they were not able to do so. Ryan is originally from there and his work and immediate family are there as well.

After getting the twins home from the hospital, Ryan planned to move with his family to Washington both for work and family support. He bought a 24-feet trailer from a dirt farmer and drove cross-country with his 5 month-old sons and wife. The journey was not a smooth one for them. After they made it to Fort Worth, Texas, he stopped to fill up gas and noticed that the wheels were not right; the axle was bent. He had to get it fixed and they were stuck in Texas for a few days for the repair.

Once the repair was done, they got going again. While driving through New Mexico during a long, hot day in the high desert, he felt something amiss. It turned out that there was smoke coming out and three out of the four tires of the trailer were blown out. The place had no phone service. It was in the middle of nowhere. They had to find some way to get help.

He managed to find a town 90 minutes away. The town was too small so he had to go to Albuquerque, which was 5 hours away. Driving through rain and winds, he managed to make it to the tire shop before they closed. He got the tires and threw them at the back of the truck and started driving back to his trailer. It was snowing in the middle of the night when they got back on the road. They made it through Death Valley, and the rain started again in Oregon and continued all the way until Washington. They were tired when they reached Washington.

He thought things would be good once they were back in Washington. He had a house there which had not been lived in for a while. He had to get some work done on the house. They lived somewhere else in the meantime till the house got ready to move in.

However, at this time, some conflicts sprung up regarding them and the house. His wife was emotionally struggling and had trouble. Ryan tried to get her psychiatric help but she resented it. She agreed to see the psychiatrist, had brain scans done and was given a 5 day per week workout plan. He thought things were improving.

Unbeknownst to him, she was planning to move back to Florida with the kids. She had become paranoid and did not want to live in Washington. She told him that she wanted to go to Florida to see her grandmother who was dying. They went via New York together and she seemed more loving. He was happy that their relationship seemed to improve. From New York, they went to Florida together and he made arrangements to work remotely to be close to his sons while he was there. He got a weird feeling while he was with them. His gut told him that something was not quite right but he brushed the thought away. That was the time when his wife and her Mom turned against him.

On July 25th, 2014, Ryan was at a parking lot in Florida. Some guy hit him with his vehicle and drove away. Thankfully, he was not hurt much. He messaged his wife, telling her that a car had hit him but she did not seem concerned at all. She told him that her mother would come to pick him up from the train station. So he got into a train to go to home. Instead of his mother-in-law coming to pick him from the train station, he received a message from her that Uncle Carlos would pick him up. Ryan could not believe it. He was trying to make sense of what was going on.

On meeting him, Uncle Carlos dropped the bombshell. He told Ryan, "Your wife and her mother have taken off with the kids and they will never let you see them again. Take your stuff but you can't stay. I can take you to a hotel." Ryan was shocked out of his life and could not believe that this was happening to him. Thankfully, all the self-development work he had done came to his rescue and instead of going into a panic, he reached out to his Tony Robbins peer group and asked for help from local people. Someone volunteered to help him out.

He felt something was amiss but was not sure

what exactly it was. He did not know what to do, had no clue where his kids were. Miami was a new place for him and he barely knew anyone over there. Luckily for him, one of the peer group members was a family law practitioner and wanted to help him out. He told him to take a train towards where he lived, picked him up from the station and gave him a place to stay.

Ryan held himself to peak state so as not to wither away. He moved, thought about happy things and did whatever he could, to not fall into despair. Since he did not have much details about what was going on, he was unable to decide the next course of action.

The attorney helped him with resources. Ryan tried to get his wife and her mother served but it was very tedious as they were going to a different house every day. Just trying to get them served was a nightmare and he had to hire a private investigator. Florida state patrol helped him and he found out that his wife had the kids' passports in the Honduras consulate. He had to get Habeas Corpus issued by Washington court for the children and tried to get the Miami court to accept it.

Initially, the sergeant told him that he might have to accept that the kids were gone but Ryan wasn't ready to accept it. He could not bear to lose his sons like this. His sons are his life!

Ryan then tried locating them with the help of Florida's State Patrol Missing Children division and hired a PI (personal investigator) as well. After a lot of effort, he was able to locate them.

Before this unexpected turn of events, Ryan had scheduled 3 months in Florida to be with his boys and their mother. That did not happen.

The Private Investigator was able to finally serve them the papers. Ryan sent the Florida police initially but they said she had a Florida order so could not help. Since they were Washington residents, Florida did not have jurisdiction so the case had to move to

Washington.

That was the Labor Day weekend and his wife was able to get dependency court in Florida to stop the case from going to Washington, imposing false allegations of abuse.

He decided to go back to Washington as everything in the law said so. While in the court there, the Washington judge said that the case would stay in Florida since the children were staying there.

Even though the dependency court found the allegations were wrong and the reason the parents were fighting was because they did not get along, Ryan was not able to bring the case back to Washington.

Family court decisions mostly depend on the judge's discretion.

Even though his children were the most important to Ryan, he could not do much till the court decided. He called out specific friends who were always there for him. He was so thankful for their support. The case continued.

In November, Ryan had signed up for his first UPW (Unleash the Power Within) seminar with Tony Robbins in San Jose, California. He was nervous about going there, afraid about something going wrong while he was away. He got to San Jose but was still not feeling like before. It took him a few hours to get there mentally. He was stressed out about what new issue he would need to handle. Thankfully, no major issue arose. Rather, he was at peace after the event.

At the event, his friend Veenu said, "Ryan, you are such an amazing father." That totally changed his state. He realized that he was not a bad father. Even though circumstances were preventing him from being with his sons physically; he was doing everything he could to be able to see them. Before this event, he wasn't sure how to deal with it psychologically.

Over the weekend, he went to meet Jorge Custino

Leonere who was such a beautiful soul, just 7 years old, who had been through chemotherapy and had only a few weeks to live. Custino told him, "I will be dying." Still she had strength. Even though she would vomit from the chemo she would turn back smiling. Her indomitable spirit inspired Ryan a lot.

In 2014, while the court battle continued to drag on, he saw his kids for the first time in around a year. He was not sure whether they would even recognize him. To his surprise, when he picked up his boy Achilus, the little one stretched up, opened his eyes and said, "Dada" again and again. Ryan will never forget the gratitude that he felt that day when he heard his son saying "dada". His efforts were bearing fruits of love.

The court had put restrictions on him to see the kids only for an hour 3 times a week. It was heart wrenching and humiliating for the father in him, but it was better than not seeing them at all. Everyone around said that he was amazing with the kids. He loved them so much. He had to go through evaluations. The results were in his favor and the outcome was that since the parents did not get along, it was a family court issue.

Fighting this legal battle to be with his sons, to be there for them as their dad, to be able to see them and get them back, Ryan burned through all his savings. He lost his money, home, retirement savings and his mother's savings too. The state gave his wife everything and she also got money from him.

Meanwhile, Ryan also lost his job. He says that at Microsoft, merely doing your job gets you fired. You have to be outstanding to survive. He was laid off from Microsoft. He had to do all the court related work himself when he did not have the money to pay an attorney.

During this ordeal, a beautiful process happened inside him. He came to manage the process, the pain, the loss without giving in to despair, without getting bitter. He forgave the mother of his kids for what she had done to him. It was more difficult for him to understand what she was doing to the children and to forgive her for that. He started realizing that more forgiveness was required. He started seeing things the way they were. He could work on his thoughts to accept the reality as it was, without any filters. He accepted and got more and more gratitude. It led him to see more beauty. It gave him peace, gave him acceptance, gave him realization.

Ryan realized that he could not change their future by fighting. Fighting or going through the court system was not the real answer. He needed to find a way to make a living which was more flexible. If he started his business and got enough money, he could be wherever he was and get representation.

It was tension or push and pain driving him when he was already in a hard place. He was fighting against another person, trying to get flexible work while dealing with it. He found tools to get help from people.

This gave him more gratitude, more heart. He was still a very achievement and outcome-oriented person. He was all about doing. Everything would be how it should be. Ryan went from acceptance to a process of introspection. He tried meditation but initially thought it was not for him. He had a self-appalled moment and then surrendered. He surrendered to the meditation. That surrender got him to a very peaceful state where he was able to forgive completely.

"Forgiveness is acceptance and I am okay with what it is". He learned to go from accepting what is, to loving what is. During this process, he continued to get to know his inner self more. He knew this stuff, but was still in his head, chasing this map.

It was frustrating to him that even if he was losing this, he loved this. He had to step up and create things.

There was so much going on, he loved his kids and he was wishing the best for them and his wife.

Eventually, once he surrendered, he saw deeper inside himself, saw judgments, growth and introspection to deeper meaning; deeper beauty to a place where he not just used these tools but found something deeper. A lasting peace, a realization of who he was, who we human beings are.

It was no longer about what he was doing but what he was becoming.

Ryan found that the more he surrendered, the more the beauty that came from his experience.

Just 3 years ago, this guy had everything. – an income of 3 hundred thousand dollars per year, a nice home, fancy cars, beautiful wife, dream trips to exotic destinations and a budding career. When life took a sudden, unexpected turn, he went from that abundance to filing bankruptcy to having a mother with cancer, to fighting a long arduous court battle to see his sons, to losing not only his savings, his house but also his retirement trying to do what really mattered (his sons) and support his family through this rough situation. He was able to see the beauty through surrender and awareness rather than just the tools and the psychology of managing the situation.

Ryan crews Tony's events whenever he can. This keeps his motivation up and keeps him going.

When you go through something so deep that cuts your spirit, and you want to thrive through it, you can only do it through love. In Rumi's words, "My heart is burning with love, all can see this flame. My heart is pulsing with passion like waves on the ocean. My friends have become strangers and I'm surrounded by enemies, but I am free as the wind, no longer hurt by those who reproach me."

Even though things go on outside of him, the circus runs completely independent of him. The court process is still going on. He chooses to stay in love and prays for the mother of his children.

During the process, he had an incredible moment. While on a business trip to Memphis to do some work with FedEx, Ryan had an entire day available at his disposal. His flight was cancelled and he was at a restaurant where he asked the bartender what to do. He was directed towards the National Museum of Civil Rights (Dr. Martin Luther King Jr.). The teaching there "Only when the sky is dark can the stars shine." hit home very profoundly for him. He then ordered a collection of Dr. King Jr.'s speeches, "Our God is Marching On".

Some key points that had a major impact on him are as follows:

"How long, not long, because the moral arch of the universe may be long, but it bends towards justice." Sermon on Jesus talking about 'Love your enemy!

"Love this. Love the person who hurts you the most. You will have opportunity to crush the enemy, don't do it. Hate the process, not the people."

Generally, people don't love their enemy. But when they do, the world opens up even more. It ceases to influence your internal world. He was also inspired by the Holocaust survivor. "I know there's bad in the world, but I want to see the beauty."

Ryan's message is that radical love is the answer. It is finding the love in yourself. Once you find your inner love, you can see the same great love the masters talked about. If you can love yourself, find love in everything, then you will find beauty in everything. You have to be willing to see it.

The illusion of separation is the cause of all suffering. Look at everything that happens as a mirror of who you are. Fall in love with what is. So much of what you do overlooks that.

"But I say to you, love your enemies, bless them that curse you, do good to them that hate you, and pray for them which spitefully use you, and persecute you"   -Matthew 5:44

For the Love of my Kids

Key Learnings:

1) Life can change any moment, live it to the fullest.

2) Change is the only constant.

3) Look at all happenings as a mirror of who you are.

4) Love is the ultimate answer.

5) A father's love for his child cannot be measured.

6) Even if you lose all material possessions, you can still live in peace.

7) Every challenge is an opportunity to grow.

8) Forgiveness will bring you peace.

9) When God gives us a dire situation, he gives us the strength to overcome it.

10) Get inspired.

11) Learn to find your happy.

12) Live in your truth.

13) Happiness comes when you accept what is, in all its entirety.

14) Hate the bad actions, not the people.

15) Love yourself and love others, even people who hurt you.

16) You can find beauty in every situation if you have the eyes to see it.

8.

Bullied to Brave

ina went to school in Los Gatos. She was a hardworking, peace loving, nerdy high schooler. She was well aware how hard her mother worked to give her a good life. Her parents had divorced when she was very young and her dad had moved to another state by the time she had started going to school. She only saw him a few times a year for a few hours. He was too busy with his job and his new family. His current wife did not encourage

Rina to visit them in Seattle.

Rina had a few friends in class with whom she liked to hang out and study. She had just turned 16 and her hormones were raging but she decided to focus on studies and was a dutiful daughter. She got good grades and the teachers always praised her abilities and her kind nature. She was easygoing and helpful.

There were some mean girls in class, two of whom were cheerleaders, Meg and Joan. They were always dressed up in the latest fashion and were the cool girls guys lusted after. There was a guy John, very handsome, well-built soccer player whom Meg wanted to have as her boyfriend. After all, she was the coolest girl in class, and deserved to be with the coolest guy there. No one else was even close, according to her.

One day, when Rina was rushing to her class lost in thoughts, with her hands full of books, she bumped into John and dropped them. He apologized and helped her pick them up. He also complemented her on getting a perfect score on the Math test. Rina had never thought that he even knew of her existence and she felt flattered.

During lunchtime he said "hi "to her with a smile. Meg saw it and got jealous. Why would he even need to acknowledge that 'dowdy gag', that 'loser'? Those were the labels these 'cool' girls used for Rina and her friends. Rina had developed a thick skin and pretended to not overhear them when they were being mean. That way, they left her alone and she had her peace.

The next day, John sat at her table to ask about some upcoming quiz and that's when Meg and Joan got totally furious, so much so that they decided to play a vicious prank on Rina. They wanted her out of their way. They invited Rina to help them study science at their house at night.

Being a helpful person who gave others the

benefit of doubt, Rina agreed to help. When her mom wanted to know if Meg's parents would be there, she said yes. So, she was relieved. Rina's friends, Melanie and Angela had warned her against Meg but Rina had a kind heart and decided to use this as an opportunity to make friends with them. After all, she thought, they were asking for help, they were trying to be friends with her. Maybe they liked her intelligence and wanted to get good grades.

When Friday night arrived, she took her books and went to Meg's house to study with the 'cool' gang. She had already finished her preparation for the upcoming exam and decided to share it with the others. When she reached there, Meg offered her a drink. Rina was surprised and asked if her parents wouldn't mind. Meg said that they were out for the weekend.

Rina was uncomfortable as her mom had made her promise not to drink alcohol till she was of legal age and she had agreed. She did not want to break her promise to her mom. She knew how hard her mom worked and how much she trusted her.

When Rina refused to drink, saying it was illegal for underage people to drink, the others started making fun of her, telling her to not be a prude, not to be a 'scared cat'. Then, some guys also came over. When Rina was teased by them all, it was too hard for her to stand her ground alone and she started drinking just to be a part of the gang, to gain their approval. She had never had alcohol before in her life, so she got drunk pretty fast. They kept on refilling her glass and it wasn't long before she passed out. That was the moment Meg and her gang were waiting for. They stripped Rina of her clothes and scribbled different 'labels' on her body with markers. Some like 'nerd', 'dowdy' and 'prude' were minor while some such as 'whore', 'slut', 'skank' and more were worse. They then took pictures of her in demeaning ways while she was still unconscious.

When Rina did not pick up the phone and it was

almost midnight, her mom got worried. She kept on calling Meg's home till Meg picked up the phone. Meg told her that they had studied so hard that Rina had fallen asleep and would be back home once she was awake. Her mom trusted her, so, she did not think anything of it. The next morning, Rina came home and locked herself in her room. When she had woken up at Meg's home, she saw the 'labels' on her body and was troubled. She felt ashamed and cried as she put on her clothes and picked up her books. She felt too embarrassed to tell her mom about the incident. She came home and locked herself in her room. Her mom asked if she wanted breakfast but she said no. Her mom thought it was just teenage moodiness and told her that breakfast was on the table, as she left for work.

Meanwhile, her friend Melanie came to visit her, worried and showed her the pictures circulating amongst her classmates. Rina was worried and upset. She made her promise not to say anything to her mom. She was devastated and stressed. She was trying to figure out what she had done to invite this sort of meanness? Why did these girls hate her so much? She did not want to go to school; she did not want to go anywhere. She just wanted to stay in her room. She did not want anyone to see her.

After a few days, when she went back to school, she could see her classmates looking at her with knowing smiles, in a demeaning way. She did not want to make eye contact with anyone, not even John. She felt ashamed, alone and unloved.

She was so done with everyone. She felt violated, she felt betrayed, and she felt worthless. The only thing which kept her from killing herself was recollecting what her gran had told her mom when her mom was falling apart after her dad had left. She had said, "No man is worth stealing the smile on my daughter's face". This had Rina think, "These girls are not worth stealing the smile on my face either. They are not as important as dad." While that thought gave her a glimmer of hope, she knew that if she did not take any action, the meanness and the bullying would continue. She had to find a smart way to stand up to them without getting bullied more.

She decided to muster the courage to tell her mom about what had happened at Meg's house. Her mom went with her to the school principal and complained about the incident, requesting him to ask other students to delete the demeaning pictures. The principal asked everyone to delete the pictures from their phones and say "sorry" to Rina for supporting her bullies. The so called 'cool' girls were put on academic probation and they had to do community service for a month.

Standing up against the bullies, Rina became a school heroine, someone all students looked up to and wanted to be like. She went on to win scholarship for her undergrad. To quote Michael J Fox who says it beautifully, "One's dignity may be assaulted, vandalized and cruelly mocked, but it can never be taken away unless it is surrendered."

You can turn any situation around and find happiness, as long as you don't give in to the victim mentality and rise beyond that. Treat challenges as an opportunity to develop strength and grit, as an opportunity to grow, to fight back, to be happy, and to create a new thought process.

"The common mistake that bullies make is assuming that because someone is nice that he or she is weak. Those traits have nothing to do with each other. In fact, it takes considerable strength and character to be a good person."

– Mary Elizabeth Williams

Bullied to Brave

Key Learnings:

1) Don't give in to peer pressure.

2) Work hard, work smart.

3) Be your child's best friend and give them freedom to discuss anything.

4) If bullying occurs, don't feel ashamed. Confide in your parents.

5) With the right emotional intelligence, you can turn any situation around.

6) Treat challenges as an opportunity to grow.

7) Develop strength, grit and determination.

8) Fight for what is right.

9) Step up, set an example.

10) Create a new thought process to find your happy.

9.

Meditation and Spirituality are the Answers

rian grew up in a family of police officers and his father was into law enforcement as well. He was always in trouble and had very low self-esteem. He used to be disciplined often and ran away from home when he was fourteen years old. He had learnt violence as a tool from his dad and found alcohol and drugs, which made it a deadly combination. He liked to fight as he enjoyed the competition. Alcohol and violence made him feel powerful and important, thus making him not feel bad about himself anymore. They also helped lower his inhibitions and made him feel bigger than he was.

He was in and out of juvenile hall till he became an adult. He worked here and there. Alcohol, drugs, guns and hustling on the streets became a regular part of his life. When he was 21 years old, he had a fight with a drug dealer, Jim Gruel, over his dog killing the latter's cat. Both were high and guns came out and Brian ended up shooting the guy to death.

He was tried in court and convicted of second degree murder, twenty-one years to life. When he went to the prison, Brian realized that he was there to die. He didn't even think that he would ever get out alive. He was put in San Quentin, the state prison for convicted felons. In his twenty-two years of prison time, he had been stationed in four different prisons.

He was well aware that lifers (prisoners convicted for life) did not get out alive in those days. Prisons are very violent. Sometimes the guards shoot the prisoners; sometimes the prisoners stab each other. Some prisoners are revictimized.

In order to keep himself safe in prison, Brian decided to use violence. He had easy access to drugs and alcohol inside the prison too and became a drug dealer himself.

In 1997, Brian's sister gave birth to a baby girl and that was a life changing moment for him. He loved his niece and wanted to leave a legacy for her. He did not want to die the same way he had come into the prison. He did not want to die getting stabbed or shot. He wanted to die differently, for his love for his niece. He decided to get sober and joined the twelve-step program for prisoners, alcoholics and narcotics anonymous.

Growing up Catholic, Brian grew up thinking that if a child is born a sinner, then why do anything different? Why not just sin some more? That way of thinking had gotten him into violence, drugs, alcohol and finally, to the prison. He was somehow different from his siblings, a little more headstrong.

After joining the 12 step program, Brian started meditating in 1998 and made it a practice to meditate twice a day, every day. That was the beginning of a whole new world for him. A world that was peaceful and non-violent, where people helped each other and were compassionate and kind. Meditation helped him calm down quite a bit and he did not feel the need to get violent to feel good about himself anymore.

His initial mediation practice was with the meditators of the Catholic Church, John of Cross. In 1999, Brian met a prison guard who was into Ananda Marga meditation. The guard inspired him with the Eastern teachings. He ended up reading the ancient Hindu scripture "Bhagwad Gita", and the philosophy totally changed his life.

The main teachings of the Gita which hit home for him, are as follows:

1) Know that the reality of the world in which you live is impermanent, unreal and the source of your suffering.

2) Know the reality about your true self, who you are and what you really are. Know that you are neither your body nor mind, but the true self that can neither be slain, nor hurt. It is eternal, divine and transcendental.

3) Know that senses are responsible for your desires, attachments and instability of the mind. By restraining your senses, you can achieve the stability of your mind and become impervious to the opposites like pain and pleasure, which is the key to self-realization.

4) Cultivate 'buddhi' or discerning knowledge to discern true knowledge and practice wisdom to know the difference between truth and untruth, reality and illusion, your true self and false self, the divine qualities and demonic qualities, knowledge and ignorance and how true knowledge illuminates and liberates

whereas ignorance veils your wisdom and holds you bondage.

5) Know the true nature of action and inaction and how actions bind you to the world and cause you suffering. Know that it is not your actions but the desires behind your actions, which are responsible for your karma. Do not seek to escape from your responsibility as not taking care of your obligatory duties is bad karma. To neutralize your karma, perform actions without desires, attachments and without seeking the fruit of your actions, as a sacrificial offering to God, accepting Him as a true doer and yourself as a mere instrument. Know that true renunciation is the renunciation of your desires and the fruit of your actions.

6) Know the Supreme Self to be all pervading and the all-knowing Creator of all. Accept him to be the cause of everything and the real doer in your life. Surrender yourself to Him completely and offer him everything that you have.

7) Cultivate the quality of 'Sattva' or purity so that you can experience the true love for God and know the true meaning of devotion, surrender and sacrifice, restraining your mind and senses and surrendering yourself to him completely. Make your life and actions as true offerings to Him, acknowledging His role in all your affairs and expressing your gratitude. If you persist in your practice, you will begin to experience total devotion to God and his unconditional love. He will take full responsibility for managing your life and manage your affairs for you.

Once he understood these Eastern teachings and philosophy, it totally changed Brian's life. But there was a conflict between the Catholic tradition and the Ananda Marga tradition which stressed him out. He discussed his dilemma with a priest who was very wise and the priest gave him the green signal to follow what resonated with him.

In June 2000, Brian met Dada Rudreshwara Nanda

and learnt tantra yoga, individual and conscious techniques and became a vegetarian. With the transformation in his mindset from violence to peace and compassion, Brian wanted to give back and help others. He started teaching the asanas (yoga poses) to his prison community to help them. He also got busy doing social service and became accountable for the prison community and the larger society he was exiled from.

He took his learnings further by reading self-development books including 'Man's search for meaning' and Baba's book. He started teaching love, loving your enemy and loving everyone. Meditation provided him with a gateway to release his pent up emotions. Once the emotions were released, he no longer had anger, thus no longer had violence. He started some meditation programs in the prison for other prisoners as well.

Meanwhile, life had a plan for him. He met the love of his life, Monica, while in prison, and also had 6 parole hearings. He was granted parole for the first time in 2009 but it was later revoked by the then Governor. In 2010, he was granted a release and got out.

When he got out after 22 years, the world was quite different. He noticed that people had changed quite a bit. They were no longer community-minded and had become more self-centered.

Brian had met Monica, the love of his life, in 2002. Before meeting her, he had never wanted a relationship or a woman, for that matter. So, initially he did not know what was happening to him, why she was always in his thoughts. It took him a while to figure out that it was love. Loving her came naturally, organically. With her, he learnt what intimacy was, just by holding hands and talking. They waited to have sex till he got out of prison till he came home. The more time they spent together, the stronger their love became. Loving her came naturally to him whereas before her, sexual conduct was more drug and alcohol induced, emotionless, just for momentary pleasure.

Brian married Monica in 2005 and they have a beautiful daughter whom they both adore. They bought a house in the mountains and are living a loving life. He not only got discharged from parole but got to vote for the first time in the last election. He has paid restitution, got himself an under grad degree and is working on his masters.

The drastic change from drugs and alcohol to meditation, spirituality and vegetarianism did not happen in one day. The process was gradual. The catalyst was the birth of his niece and the change was slow. When he joined the 12 Step Program, he was skeptical and did not believe that it would work but decided to give it a try anyways. When it started working and he stopped taking drugs and alcohol, he had the moral dilemma about drug trafficking. He still believed that even if he did not do drugs, he would still die in prison. He couldn't sell out who he was. He had a reputation for violence and he was tough and strong. He took some other guys with him to the meditation and yoga sessions. He started doing things differently in the prison. He mentored his friend Kenny to become a yoga instructor once the latter was released from the prison.

Brian's transformation was phenomenal. He likes to give back to the community. He works with other addicts and speaks about how meditation helped him change for the better. His message is that he hopes that the addicts are broken enough to get all the way in without being stopped and hitting rock bottom. He hopes that they come all the way in and do whatever it takes to change, that they are hungry enough, that they have the gift of desperation.

Brian believes in miracles happening every day. When he started being grateful instead of being entitled, his life changed drastically. Instead of dying in prison, dying as a convict, he is living the American dream.

Prisons are way over crowded and there is barely breathing space. So, his message is:

1) Have enough hunger
2) Be ready for change
3) Pressure makes you grow
4) Be okay with whatever life brings
5) The mind is the only thing which keeps us imprisoned
6) Don't indulge in victim mentality

In spite of being incarcerated at 21, Brian does not regret the experience as that made him the man he is today. He is fulfilled, happy and knows that everything happens when the time is right. He realizes that people who are hurt themselves, hurt other people. He helps prisoners have a better life.

"Meditation is meeting eternity in the present moment. It is resolving every problem as it comes. It is resolving every tension as it creeps in. It is facing the challenges of life in a non-fearful way." ~Vimala Thakar

Meditation and Spirituality are the Answers

Key Learnings:

1) Meditation and spirituality can work wonders.

2) Love can change anyone for the better.

3) Accept life and be ready for change.

4) Having a gratitude mindset makes your life better.

5) Pressure makes you grow.

6) Drugs, alcohol and violence are never the answers; peace and love are the answers.

7) It's never too late to live your dream life.

8) Intimacy is more than just sex.

9) Giving back makes you fulfilled.

10) The mind is the only thing that keeps us in prison.

11) Everything comes when the time is right.

10.
CANCER FREE AND THRIVING

Audrey Levan is an actress, model and mother to a 26 year old daughter. She has a background as a resource person and tutor for special needs children. Apart from acting, she is also passionate about helping children.

In 2005, life was going well for Audrey till it threw a curve ball. She had a beautiful family, a nice house and a fulfilling career, working with special needs children. One day while she was in the shower, she felt a lump in her right breast. She was concerned and wanted to get it checked out. She called the hospital and asked to be referred to a surgeon and made an appointment. When she met with the surgeon, following the protocol, he wanted to start the tests, beginning with a mammogram. Her gut told her to ask for a biopsy instead and she was able to convince him to prescribe it. Within a week, the diagnosis came in and it was what she was afraid of! She had two lumps in her breast and the bigger lump was malignant, in other words, she had breast cancer.

Being a highly spiritual, rational and calm person, she decided to not let panic set in as she shared the dreadful news with her family. Everyone was concerned for her and her sister started crying and feeling sorry for her. Audrey wanted to remain positive and asked her to not feel pity and be positive around her. She wanted to be strong for her daughter. She prayed to God to take care of her daughter, should something happen to her and she was no longer around.

Even though the lumps were malignant, the smaller one was in the early stage and the bigger one was in the second stage. Also, the cancer had not spread to the lymph node. So, she did not need mastectomy and lumpectomy was performed instead.

Some details about mastectomy and lumpectomy are as follows:

Mastectomy: It is the surgical removal of the complete breast and is advised under the following conditions:

1) Cancer has spread to the lymph node.
2) Peace of mind for patients that chances of recurrence are less.
3) Not wanting radiation.

The disadvantages of mastectomy are that it is more expensive and results in the permanent loss of the breast. It is usually followed by breast reconstruction surgery. Radiation might still be needed, depending on the pathology.

Lumpectomy: The surgery only removes the lumps from the breast. The main advantage is that the sensation and appearance of the breast can be preserved. Comparatively, it is less invasive than mastectomy and has a shorter recovery time.

- The main disadvantage is that it is usually followed by five to seven weeks of radiation, five days per week, after lumpectomy surgery, to make sure the cancer is gone.

- Radiation therapy may also affect the timing of reconstruction and possibly reconstruction options after surgery.

Audrey had to go for chemo for four times, once every three weeks. The chemo made her body very weak and she had to be in bed 3 to 4 days after each session. She could not eat much and the taste in her mouth was so bad that she felt like throwing up all the time, for the first few days after each chemo session. She relied on her spirituality and faith to get through this tough time. She believed that it is up to us how we respond to life. Life will make you fall, how you react is the choice you have.

She lost her hair from chemo but did not let that affect her self-image. One time while she was at Starbucks in a jeans and T-shirt and bald head, a young kid started playing with her. The kid's mother could only see her back. The mother asked the kid to stop playing with the gentleman and disturbing him as he was waiting for his coffee. When Audrey turned her head, the lady felt embarrassed to have called her a guy and apologized profusely.

2005 was a tough year for Audrey. Not only was she diagnosed with breast cancer, but also lost someone she was very close to, her mother. She was distraught and cried a lot. Her spirituality helped her cope with both catastrophes in her life. Even when she did not know what the outcome would be or how long she would live, her only concern was the welfare of her daughter who is the apple of her eye. She prayed to God to take care of her daughter very well and keep her happy, even when she was not there. She was accepting of the cancer and whatever God brought her way. She let the divine lead her, in full acceptance of the guidance.

Another event that made her very emotional was that her favorite TV anchor, Peter Jennings was also diagnosed with lung cancer at the same time that she was diagnosed with breast cancer. He passed away three months after the diagnosis. She cried a lot after hearing about it. That made her realize how flimsy life can be.

The cancer was a wakeup call for her to take care of herself. She quit smoking and started incorporating healthy habits in her daily routine. She also realized the flimsiness of life and started living each day fully. Her marriage hadn't been working for a while because of differences and she and her husband decided to file for divorce. It was finalized, the following year.

Cancer became the catalyst for her to take her life in her own hands and start living for herself too, not just for others. In order to do that, she had to make the tough decision. They agreed that the marriage wasn't working out for them and both of them would be happier with someone else.

She became more spiritual, more positive. more compassionate and became cancer free. She identifies herself with Phoenix rising from the ashes. She feels more alive, more powerful and more beautiful than before. Post cancer, she has long, thick wavy hair, that she loves. She never had wavy hair before.

She moved out in 2006 and started living on her own, living life on her terms and hasn't looked back since. She had always wanted to become an actress, so took acting classes and followed her passion. Through her acting, she wants to send the message of love to humanity. She says, "If you want to live with dignity, you have to serve others." She wants the readers to be aware that life can be taken away any day. So, don't live in the past, as it will depress you.

Don't live in the future, as it will make you anxious. The only thing you have is the present. If you want to live in peace with yourself, live in the moment. You will be at peace with the world as well.

In the words of Leo Tolstoy, "There is only one time, that is important. NOW! It is the most important time as it is the only time that we have any power."

Cancer Free and Thriving

Key Learnings:

1) Smoking is not good for you.

2) Adopt a healthy lifestyle.

3) Keep your calm.

4) Positive attitude helps you heal better.

5) The only time you have is the present.

6) Follow your passion.

7) Life is too short to be unhappy.

8) Don't wait too long in bad relationships.

9) Be with someone who makes you feel alive.

10) Help the less fortunate.

11) Life is flimsy. It can end in a moment. No one is guaranteed a tomorrow.

12) Be at peace.

13) Spirituality makes you calm.

11.

Mentally Challenged to Happy

Michael grew up in Chicago in a not so well to do, big family. He is the oldest amongst his 5 siblings. His parents had kids while still young. They had five kids by the time they were twenty-seven years old. Currently, he is 56 years old of age but has the brain of an eight-year-old.

Growing up, his parents were never willing to accept his developmental challenges, because of ignorance and fear. They decided to treat him like a normal child, afraid that if people knew about his developmental challenge, he would be taken away from them. As a result, he had a frustrating and unfulfilling life, pretending to be normal in a world that could not see him for who he truly was. He never read beyond the capability of an eight-year-old. Necessary help, lifestyle skills, emotional, physical and monetary support were denied to him until two years ago when his only surviving parent passed away in 2014.

His second sibling and younger sister always knew of his challenges. Throughout the years, the sister wanted to help him lead a fulfilling life but did not have the family's support to do so. The reason being that they would have to admit neglect if they agreed to get him the help. Whenever she tried to bring up the issue, she was rebuffed that he was not retarded. They did not realize the difference between being retarded and being mentally challenged. The sister was aware that he needed assistance and that he was not retarded. She knew that without assistance he was merely surviving, not really living. He was overweight and diabetic.

When Michael was 12 years old, he worked in a neighborhood shoe shop, stocking shelves. The owner used to play hide and seek with him and took advantage of his limited intellect and eventually raped him, in the guise of playing with him. Michael did not fully comprehend what had happened. As Michael did not understand the full impact of what had happened, the shoe shop owner was not confronted. This made him very frustrated and depressed, resulting in every little thing setting him off emotionally and making him cry.

Michael now knows that people learn in different ways. Even he did not want to admit that he had limits to his learning. He was very angry when, after a high school test, they said that he only had the knowledge of a third grader. He knew that genetically or chemically, something was not quite right; his motor skills were not so good and there was a lack of coordination.

When he was growing up, there was no special education available for kids with special needs. The special needs kids were put in a home for the mentally retarded. His parents did not want that to happen to him. His father worked very hard to support the 7 members of his family. His mother had health issues for most of her adult life.

When he was nineteen years old, he started dating a girl whom he thought was his soul mate. She was a stripper at a local joint, Cabby store. Although he knew that she worked there, he was under the impression that it was a cab place, until one day, he went to her work place and found out that she was a stripper. He started working at that strip club, cleaning up and being a security guard to escort the strippers to bachelor parties.

In one of the bachelor parties he went to with her, he found out that those were the people he had grown up with. He asked her to not accept bachelor parties from people he knew but she had a mind of her own and would not listen. This young woman knew of no other type of life, no other way to support herself. Her own father had sent her to work at the strip club when she was just 15. She was a rape victim herself.

Because of his mental disability, she took advantage of him and stole all his money. He felt so betrayed that he wanted to kill her. Luckily for him, he fell asleep after drinking tequila, while waiting for her to get home.

During this timeframe, he was able to find out the address of the perpetrator who had raped him when he was a kid. Michael went to his house and beat him to a pulp. The guy would have died if the onlookers hadn't called the cops. When the cops asked him why he was beating the man up, he told them the reason and had their sympathy.

His life was in bad shape till he was 24 years old. He washed dishes in a restaurant and ate whatever food they had, thus gaining a lot of weight. He met a priest, Father Cook, when he was twenty-five years old and the father influenced him to change his ways a little and start going to church.

After the incident with the rapist, his uncle invited him to Florida to work in a restaurant. He lived there for a couple of years before moving back to Chicago to be near his family. His mother always encouraged him to live a normal life. That's how he started working in the restaurant. He had jobs where he would live in a room at the establishments that he worked.

Once his parents passed away, his sister was able to finally get him the necessary help in order for him to lead a happy life. He was 54 years old at this time. He started his life all over again at 54 and this was the beginning of a totally different world for him, where he sees life in a positive way and wants to help others. He now accepts himself for who he is and knows that it is okay not to be "normal". He is happy that he is not just surviving but thriving now. His sister has hired a wellness coach to do house checkups and ensure he is able to live a semi-independent life safely. She also created a picture budget for Michael so that the wellness coach can check and ensure that he is dividing his money into the different expenditures. For example, one envelope is for the puppy, one for the doctor, one for groceries and so on.

He is comfortable enough with living in Texas after learning some life skills with her help. He has another sister close by. He likes the people around him in Texas as they do not treat him like a retard. The wellness coach looks after him and helps him manage his money and develop healthy habits. He has lost 90 LBs in 1 year and has not gained any weight back. His weight is down from 367LBs to 276LBs. He works out every day and eats healthy food. The result has been phenomenal for his health. He is no longer diabetic; his cholesterol and acid reflux are well under control.

Michael is in physical therapy and is learning to live well after his big toe had to be amputated due to an infection, which wouldn't heal because of diabetes. Whenever he doesn't want to go to the gym or feels lazy, he looks at the big toe and that gives him enough motivation.

Some of his old friends are no longer his friends as they believe in pity parties and did not like him changing for the better. He does not like hanging out with negative people so that he is able to keep the positive change. He has a puppy, which works wonders for his mood. Even when he has had a really bad day, the puppy is able to make him happy within a few minutes. He also has stopped being so angry and is able to calm down quickly. He has stopped repeating the same record over and over again and says that the true definition of crazy is playing the same record and expecting a different result. That's a really insightful learning!

One of the major learnings Michael now has, is that things will happen in your life, no matter what. Don't let it get into your soul and your mind because if you get it inside your mind, it will stay a long time. He no longer gives in to fear. He has become confident and is learning to cook new dishes and wants to help mentor kids.

"It isn't what you have, or who you are, or where you are, or what you are doing that makes you happy or unhappy. It is what you think about."

-Dale Carnegie

Mentally Challenged to Happy

Key Learnings:

1) It's never too late to get the help you need and start living.

2) Developmentally challenged people can become independent with the right support.

3) Don't be afraid to get the necessary help for your child.

4) It's never too late to start being happy and healthy.

5) Don't indulge in a pity party.

6) When you make positive changes, negative people will not stay.

7) Life will happen; it's up to you, how you react.

8) Don't judge; be compassionate towards the less fortunate.

9) Healthy habits lead to a healthy life.

10) Healthy life helps you find your happy.

11) Working out and eating healthy will lead to finding your happy.

12) Don't give in to fear and find something you like to do.

13) Don't expect different results if you keep on doing the same things.

HAVING A POSITIVE MINDSET HELPS!

12.
LONELY & MISUNDERSTOOD

I t's so easy to say, be happy! Jiya was thinking, it's a whole other thing to be really happy.

Jiya was feeling sorry for herself since she thought that no one really understood her, not even her closest friends and family. "They really have no clue what I am going through", she thought. "It's the worst feeling in the world when the one you love, does not love you back. My heart is breaking into pieces and all they can tell me is - be happy. Happy, my foot! They haven't gotten their heart broken, what do they know what it feels like!"

She was feeling really down, was very despondent and negative about her situation. The guy she was in love with, CJ, was not showing any interest in her. The last time she saw him at school, he was with another beautiful girl, deep in conversation. When she felt the pang of jealousy seeing them together, she knew that she had very deep feelings for him. Otherwise, she would not care.

She hadn't felt that way for anyone before, even her first guy, the one she had thought she would get married to. When she had met him, she had thought that he was the one. They had an instant attraction and got along really well. They had been together for two years but after the initial bout of passion, seemed to not feel it anymore. They seemed to have lost the mojo and it had dawned upon both of them that they were better off as friends than lovers.

After a few weeks, this new guy CJ had joined her class and there was something about him that made her think about him a lot, that made her heart race.

She felt very attracted to him, more than she had ever felt and hoped that he felt the chemistry too. She was shy, even though she was a straight A student. She tried to get his attention in subtle ways. Every time the teacher asked a question, she was the first one to raise her hand, hoping that he would notice her.

To make matters worse, now CJ was surrounded by the other pretty girls in the class. He seemed to make them laugh a lot, and they seemed to enjoy his company.

One of the days, while Jiya was walking home from school, she saw a dog on the other side of the road. She did not pay much attention to it and kept on walking. Suddenly, the dog rushed towards her, hurled his body against her leg and took a portion of flesh from her legs in his mouth and made a circle, as if to bite her again. She was afraid that he might attack again and limped away as fast as she could, towards the corner where she could see other people. Her legs were bloody, and tears were streaming down her face. Thankfully, she did not panic too much. She sat on the curb and called 911 and also called her friends. The ambulance and police arrived within a few minutes and she was taken to emergency where they said that she might need to take a rabies shot if the dog had not been given the shots. The dog did not have a collar on him, so most likely, might not have had the rabies shot.

Even though they said she needed the shots, the funny thing was that the nurse informed her about a shortage of rabies shots and unless the dog showed signs of madness, while in the compound, they would not be able to give her the rabies shot. Having heard that the rabies shots were really painful, Jiya wasn't too excited about taking them anyway and was happy that she did not have to take any. They also put her on antibiotics. By the time they put bandages on her wounds, her had friends arrived, worried about her.

Since CJ started attending her class, she wanted to look beautiful to get CJ's attention. She had gotten new highlights and trendy clothes. She couldn't wear those now though as she had to go to school on crutches - with big bandages on her legs. The antibiotics were making her tummy hurt. She became quiet and despondent. Her friends thought that she was down because of the injury and tried to cheer her up by telling her that within a couple of months, she would heal and get back to normal. She knew that and wasn't in the least concerned about recovering. Her heart was hurting for CJ's attention. Why doesn't he show some concern? Why doesn't he ask about the injury?

"If he liked me at all, he would have asked, she thought." To her it felt as if her life was over, meaningless without him. Once, he did come to ask about her leg. But, she was so terrified that he would guess how she felt that she was unusually curt with him, and he left. That put her even more down. She became quite moody, so much that even her friends didn't want to hang around her for long. That alone time had her go frequently to the library and read a lot. She also started writing a journal daily. That helped her express how she really felt and expressing her feelings on paper, lessened some of the sadness she felt inside.

She started reading Dale Carnegie's book 'How to stop worrying and start living' and one of the main takeaways from the book for her was to assign a specific amount of time to worrying, and she gave herself 30 minutes per day to worry, no more, no less. If she still felt sorry for herself after that time, she got herself busy and that got her mind off of him.

Once she was able to practice assigning a time to worry, she started becoming her old cheerful self again, and as she healed, she had a new insight and a new understanding towards others. She won the **'Student of the Year'** award that year. She also learnt some meditation and easy yoga poses to help her healing. That helped her become calm, centered and grounded. That made her look more beautiful, so much so that CJ not only noticed her but also asked her out on a date and later to the prom.

"Decide in your heart of hearts what really excites and challenges you, and start moving your life in that direction. Every decision you make, from what you eat to what you do with your time tonight, turns you into who you are tomorrow, and the day after that. Look at who you want to be, and start sculpting yourself into that person. You may not get exactly where you thought you'd be, but you will be doing things that suit you in a profession you believe in. Don't let life randomly kick you into the adult you don't want to become."

-Chris Hadfield

Lonely & Misunderstood

Key Learnings:

1) People perceive others according to how their viewpoint.

2) If you feel misunderstood, explain so others would understand.

3) Sometimes, blessings come disguised as problems.

4) Reading helps widen your horizon.

5) When you are grounded, you have more gravity.

6) Worrying takes away your happiness.

7) Assigning specific time to worry, helps reduce it.

8) Understanding others helps you also understand yourself.

13.

Find Your Happy

Just as Brian, Ryan, Audrey, Rina and others found happiness in spite of major challenges in their lives, so can you. Finding genuine happiness is possible. Life is not happening to you; it's happening for you. Our attitude and the decisions we make ultimately decides the quality of our lives. In order to find lasting happiness, it is very important to not give in to a pity party and incorporate positive habits and rituals in our daily lives, which will help us develop the foundation to find our happy in every situation, whatever life brings. Some of the key learnings from the life stories which will help us lay the foundation are as follows:

Key Learnings to Find Your Happy

1) *Barriers to Love*

i)   Don't be afraid to fall in love.

ii) One bad experience is a very small sample.

iii) Every relationship helps you learn and grow.

iv) Learn to heal from heartbreak.

v)   Don't rush from one relationship to another, give yourself time to heal.

vi) You can build anything from nothing.

vii) There is a purpose to everyone who enters your life.

viii) Not everyone can feel as deeply as you.

ix) It takes courage to fall in love again.

x)   The right person will love you back.

2) *Living in Fear*

i)   Living in fear is the antidote to happiness.

ii) Facing your fears leads to happiness.

iii) Marriage of convenience is not a happy marriage.

iv) Getting out of the comfort zone is the key to happiness.

v) Don't trust someone who betrayed you once, no matter how sweet they are.

vi) Get into spirituality and self-development.

vii) Seek counseling when you are in a narcissistic relationship. Don't try to handle a narcissist alone.

3) *Control and Codependence*

i) It's not your fault when someone abuses you and your trust.

ii) You are the only one who can put yourself first.

iii) Don't let others take advantage of your kindness.

iv) Seek counseling and help.

v) Don't be ashamed to tell family and friends about the abuse.

vi) Don't be too naive.

vii) No one is worth stealing the smile from your face.

viii) Help others.

ix) Be kind to only those who deserve it, not to those who use it.

4) *Duh to Disability*

i)   Trust your gut feeling, no matter what the diagnosis.

ii) Find ways to feel inspired.

iii) Read the side effects of your medications.

iv) Focus on the end goal.

v)   Don't let what others tell you doubt your recovery.

vi) Visualize a strong and healthy you.

vii) If you are determined to heal, you will.

5) *Entitlement to Maturity*

i)   Entitlement is an antidote to happiness.

ii) Don't always give in to your kids' tantrums.

iii) Teach good values to your kids which will help them once they grow up.

iv) Learn to be happy with simple things.

v)   Get rid of drama and expectation.

vi) Don't be too selfish. Think about other people's happiness as well.

6) *For the Love of my kids*

i) Narcissism causes havoc to those around you.
ii) Choosing love over bitterness brings joy, no matter what.
iii) A father's love for his kids cannot be measured. It's as deep as the ocean.
iv) Self-development helps in dealing with life's challenges.
v) Challenges make you grow.
vi) Good people always try to help.
vii) If you feel about something strongly, don't give up.

7) *Bullied to Brave*

i) Stand up to bullies.
ii) Being bullied is not your fault.
iii) Don't give in to weakness or self-pity when you are bullied.
iv) Become strong and get the teacher's and others' help.

v) Understand the bully's psychology and that will help to better deal with them.

vi) Find out the bully's weakness.

vii) Don't be afraid. It will be worth standing up to them.

viii) Once you stand up for yourself, your confidence will multiply.

8) Meditation and Spirituality are the answers

i) Children need to feel loved, no matter how much trouble they cause.

ii) Violence is never the answer.

iii) Drugs and alcohol provide only momentary pleasure, never long term.

iv) Meditation changes people's thought process.

v) Spirituality changes how you feel about yourself.

vi) When you heal, your life transforms.

vii) Intimacy is more than sex.

viii) Gratitude transforms the quality of your life.

ix) Happiness is possible for everyone, even if you are incarcerated, as long as you have it in you to change.

x) Helping others in need, brings fulfillment.

9) Cancer Free & Thriving

i) Keep a positive attitude.

ii) Spirituality helps you from panicking.

iii) Have faith.

iv) Take care of yourself and get rid of unhealthy habits.

v) Keep a positive outlook no matter what life throws at you.

vi) Do what you have always wanted to do.

vii) Have a gratitude mindset.

viii) If a relationship is not working out, leave.

ix) Live every day to its fullest. No one is promised tomorrow.

10) *Mentally Challenged to Happiness*

i) It's never too late to have a new beginning.

ii) You are never too old to start living.

iii) There is a time and place for everything.

iv) Don't hold grudges.

v) Don't let sexual abuse stop you from living your life.

vi) Family has your back.

11) Lonely & Misunderstood

1) People perceive others according to how their viewpoint.

2) If you feel misunderstood, explain so others would understand.

3) Sometimes, blessings come disguised as problems.

4) Reading helps widen your horizon.

5) When you are grounded, you have more gravity.

6) Worrying takes away your happiness.

7) Assigning specific time to worry, helps reduce it.

8) Understanding others helps you also understand yourself.

In order to find out your current state and what you need to be happy, please answer the following questions. Don't dwell too much on them. Take a few minutes to answer.

I) Questions to Ask Yourself

-Why am I feeling_____?

-Where does this lead?

-How it affects me and those around me?

-Does this make me feel better or worse?

-How can I change how I feel?

-Do I need to talk to someone?

-Do I need to write?

-Do I need to hear music?

-Do I need to go outside?

-Will a walk in nature help?

-Do I need to move or dance?

-Do I love myself?

-Am I confident or do I compare myself with others?

-If yes, how do I feel when I compare?

-Do I ever appreciate myself?

-What do I feel good about?

Happiness is a feeling, an emotion, everyone wants and everyone deserves in order to experience joy. When we are young and innocent, we are happy at the smallest things. As a child, if you get a new toy, someone to play with or get fed, you are happy. As we grow older, our needs and desires increase and it takes much more to be happy. Sometimes, either life happens or our wants become unrealistic or we lose hope. That makes us unhappy. Some get depressed, some get angry, some get frustrated, and some get jealous. When any of these emotions become predominant in our lives, we forget to be happy, we lose our happy.

The question then arises; how do we find our happy once we have lost it? Sometimes people say, it isn't as easy as it sounds. You don't know what I have been through. But then, if you saw what the people in the previous stories went through, you realize that compared to that, your life was a bed of roses. It all depends on our perception.

Also, you get inspired by their example, by their grit, their determination, their strength. When you are unhappy, ask yourself these questions:

1) If these people can find happiness in spite of life happening, why can't you? What if life was not happening to you, but happening for you?

2) What are the things in your life you are grateful for?

3) If they didn't let life stop them, why should you?

4) If they found a way out of the weakness of the victim mentality, why can't you?

5) What routine did they need to follow, what changes did they need to make to find their happy?

6) What is it that is keeping you from finding your happy?

7) What habits are keeping you from finding your happy?

8) What habits (both mental and physical) do you need to develop in order to be happy?

9) What excuses are stopping you from finding your happy?

10) How do you relate to others? Are you competitive or collaborative?

11) What are your top basic human needs? How are they helping or harming you?

12) What emotional conditioning keeps you from finding your happy? Is it fear? Is it anger? Is it grudge? Is it feeling unworthy? Is it feeling unloved? Or is it jealousy because some people have more than you? Think about it and write it down.

13) What are you losing out on by not being happy?

14) How do you live your life when you are happy?

15) What do you need to learn to find your happy?

16) What do you need to unlearn to find your happy?

17) How is your lifestyle keeping you from finding your happy?

18) What changes do you need to make in your environment to find your happy?

19) What does it take to lose your happy? Is it a big thing or a small thing?

20) What steps do you need to take to find your happy?

14.

Steps to finding your treasure, your happy:

1) When you create a plan A, also create plan B, C and D in case A does not work out.

2) Create your goal – No matter what, you will find your treasure, you will find your happy.

3) Look at your answers from the questions above and summarize the key points. Those key points will help you develop your clues to finding your treasure (your happy).

4) Make a deadline, a timeframe to when you will find your treasure.

5) Decide how you will reward yourself when you find the treasure. Have small rewards for each

clue which takes you closer to your treasure, and a big reward after you find the treasure.

6) Have your eye on the end goal, not on the pirates (obstacles) on the way to the treasure. (This is to ensure that you don't get disheartened if things don't go as planned)

7) Find an accountability partner or a coach to keep you on track.

8) Instead of having expectations, appreciate what you have.

9) Take ownership for your life.

10) Your decisions decide the quality of your life.

11) Incorporate the following on a regular basis:

- Gratitude: Be grateful for at least five things every morning.

- Random acts of kindness: Be kind to at least two people you don't like, every week.

- Exchange expectation for appreciation.

- Read something which inspires you, every day.

- Declutter: your mind and your environment to make room for happy.
- Try appreciating something in everyone, especially those closest to you.
- Help the less fortunate. That will help you put things in perspective.
- Get rid of the toxins in your life. Whether it's a toxic thought, toxic pattern, toxic relationship or toxic friendship.
- Make a list of what you will and won't tolerate in your life.
- Create a daily ritual
- Incorporate healthy habits: healthy eating, working out, meditation, prayers, spirituality.
- Don't indulge in pity parties, however tempting it might be.
- Hang out with positive people.
- Watch comedies.
- Incorporate soothing music, chanting, dancing and movement into your daily life.

- Do something for yourself.

- Realize that happiness comes from within.

- Decide how much time you will give yourself
  to feel sorry when life happens (3 to 30
  minutes is ideal).

- When life throws a curve ball, learn to ace the
  batting.

- Live in the present. Past can't be changed and
  future is not promised to anyone.

- Look in the mirror every day and tell yourself
  how much you love you.

- Everything happens for a reason. Sometimes
  hardships and trauma bring out our
  strength and make us unstoppable.

- Get out of your comfort zone. Get rid of
  unnecessary rules from your life.

- Stop comparing yourself to others. You are
  unique.

- Find out what gives you fulfillment and focus
  on it.

- Learn the art of self- discipline, self-
   preservation and self-love.

   Remember, you are a result of the decisions
you made, not a victim of the circumstances. In
words of Carl Jung, "You are not what
happened to you, but you are what you chose
to become." So, make the decision to find your
happy, no matter what life throws at you. The
strength to do is already within you, all you
need to do is to tap into it. Life is more fun
when we learn to make lemonade and spice it
up a little. So that when life throws us lemons,
we can not only make lemonade, but have
some fun while doing that.

   Don't expect someone else to bring you
happiness. You are the owner of your
happiness! Once you accept and love who you
are totally, you will be able to find your happy.
Being happy doesn't depend on what you own,

what kind of a house you live in, what's your career, what's your family background or who is your significant other. Being happy comes from appreciating what you have and loving yourself.

Happiness comes from inside, not from outside. When you live in love, when you live in gratitude, when you live in appreciation, then you will find your happy. In the words of Mahatma Gandhi, *"Happiness is when what you think, what you say and what you do, are in harmony."*

"Success is not the key to happiness. Happiness is the key to success. If you love what you are doing, you will be successful." Herman Cain

Gratitude!!!

I am grateful for my loving family,
Grateful for my friends,
The ones who were a lesson
The ones on whom
Everyone depends...

I am grateful for the beauty,
Trust, confidence and passion
Love, support, faith,
Kindness & compassion.

Grateful for the opportunities,
Abundance, fortune, prosperity,
Angels watching over, blessings,
Thoughtfulness & generosity.

Thankful for the universe
Watching over my back,
Courage strength, rationality
Moving forward,
Not looking back.

About the Author:

Visionary, Entrepreneur, High Tech Executive, Speaker, Happiness Coach, and Chief Strategist & Founder, Happiness Factor LLC. Anita Kumari Srivastava has a magnitude of talents. She has a MBA background and a quest for empowering both individuals and organizations to happiness, motivation and joy. She is a certified NLP, Hypnotherapy and MER practitioner and believes that happiness is everyone's birth right.

She was born in India and lives in the US. Apart from being an award winning poetess and coach, she has also starred in Zumba videos and plays. When life threw her a few curve balls, she decided to ace her batting skills and learnt the skills to find happiness. Her passion is to share those techniques with others and enable them to find happiness as well.

She loves to crew Tony's events and runs her own inspirational meetup in the Silicon Valley. She likes to get rid of at least one fear every year. She loves to walk on fire, climb mountains and strategize.

Her numerous hobbies include cooking healthy, flavorful food, dancing, hiking, working out, kickboxing, modeling, reading, writing, golfing and self-development.

She loves to volunteer and help the less fortunate and

dreams of helping poor girls in developing countries get educated and not be forced into prostitution.

Her startup Happiness Factors LLC (www.happinessfactors.com) empowers people and organizations to happiness. It provides inspirational talks, one on one coaching sessions as well as happiness seminars.

I would like to end by sharing a short poem:

"Joyous thoughts
Create a playful outlook.
Playful outlook creates
A positive demeanor.
Positive demeanor
Creates happy experiences.
Happy experiences
Make life a celebration."

Find your happy! Make your life a CELEBRATION!

For comments and feedback regarding this book, please email: findhappy14U@gmail.com

Audrey Levan: Cancer Free and Thriving

Anita Srivastava

Michael: Mentally Challenged to Happy

Anita Srivastava

Key Websites:

-For Free Happy Bonuses, please visit:

WWW.FINDYOURHAPPYBOOK.COM

-To Know More About Happiness Factor, please visit

WWW.HAPPINESSFACTORS.COM

Made in the USA
San Bernardino, CA
06 February 2017